PRAISE FOR
THE REVENUE ACCELERATOR

"Having launched a few start-ups of my own, and as a serial entrepreneur, I wish I would have had access to this information much earlier in my career. The 21 Boosters that Allan guides us through in this amazing book are spot-on for anyone looking to launch a start-up or reinvigorate an existing business."

—Michael Norton,
CEO and Founder, Tramazing

"Dr. Allan Colman has hit the nail on the head with *The Revenue Accelerator*. He brings together diverse perspectives and common, practical themes gained by people who have actual first-hand experiences as entrepreneurs in an organized and easy-to-understand way. These perspectives will be of immeasurable value to people who are ready to go for the brass ring."

—Steven M. Venokur,
Founder and Managing Partner, People Sciences, Inc.

"Sometimes you have to go slow to go fast. And this book will show you how."

—Karen Mangia,
WSJ Bestselling Author and Salesforce Executive

"This is a book every start-up owner needs. Step by step, it tells you how to get it right. Get it, read it, keep it handy for reference."
—Don Davis,
The Capital Raise Lawyer

"Around the globe, entrepreneurship is the way forward for changing life's trajectory in a positive way, yet there are many pitfalls. Wouldn't it make sense to have a guide to increase the likelihood of success multifold? *The Revenue Accelerator* provides that entrepreneurial roadmap."
—Jeff Rogers,
Chairman, OneAccord; Founder,
Legato Equity, KIROS, Solomons Fund

"*The Revenue Accelerator* is a book every organization can use to drive results. If you are looking for a new approach to succeed in today's complex marketplace, look no further."
—Scott Hogle,
President of iHeartMedia Honolulu
and Bestselling Author of *PERSUADE*

"Since 1987, when Allan Colman helped us launch our non-profit start-up, The Children's Cancer Research Fund, it has contributed several million dollars for initial clinical trials of new therapies and treatments. His book is full of techniques and tactics that will help non-profits as well as for-profit start-ups who are serious about making their service successful."
—Stephen Contopulos,
Director/Secretary, Children's Cancer Research Fund

"This book is a critical tool for start-up entrepreneurs who are serious about taking their new product to market. It teaches how to finance, market, sell and overcome bumps in the road."

—Lloyd M. Johnson Jr,
CEO, Chief Legal Executive LLC

"This book is the necessary guide for the 100% of start-ups that want to succeed in an environment where only 20% will. If you want to beat those long odds, read this book."

—Richard Levick,
Chairman and CEO, LEVICK

"Not only is the information current and relevant, but the tools and lists provided throughout will be a godsend for any person trying to start a business. My hat is off to Dr. Colman, and I know that whoever picks up his book will be that much closer to a successful business launch—which is truly extraordinary in this post-pandemic world!"

—Debbie Goldfarb,
Owner, BIZ Made EZ;
Small Business Development
Advisor, El Camino College

THE REVENUE ACCELERATOR

The 21 Boosters to Launch Your Start-Up

DR. ALLAN COLMAN

MADE FOR
SUCCESS

Made for Success Publishing
P.O. Box 1775 Issaquah, WA 98027
www.MadeForSuccessPublishing.com

Distributed by Made for Success Publishing

First Printing

Library of Congress Cataloging-in-Publication data

Colman, Allan
    The Revenue Accelerator: The 21 Boosters to Launch
    Your Start-Up
        p. cm.

LCCN: 2022905611
ISBN: 978-1-64146-718-6 *(Paperback)*
ISBN: 978-1-64146-719-3 *(eBook)*
ISBN: 978-1-64146-727-8 *(Audiobook)*

Printed in the United States of America

For further information contact Made for Success Publishing
+14255266480 or email service@madeforsuccess.net

Contents

Dedication

To Dan, Gail and Paul:
I hope you are looking down from above and smiling.

To all the "Cowboys" and the "Pi Lambers":
We still ride together.

To Robin: My love always.

INTRODUCTION

66Opportunities are like buses; if you miss one, another will be coming along.99
—Sir Richard Branson

I WAS NEVER TAUGHT how to sell. But by going through the struggles, obstacles, roadblocks, challenges, wrong turns, and searching for real opportunities, my self-education took hold. I wrote *The Revenue Accelerator* to help you avoid many of the problems start-up entrepreneurs experience in making the leap from building their product or service to selling it.

During my first career in city and county management, I was often presenting programs that required tough decisions that impacted services to residents and businesses. I gave elected officials opportunities to support as well as challenge the recommendations. Sitting in open public meetings while taking criticism was very tough. It took a highly seasoned human resources director, Bill Wagstaff, to teach me the value of "pre-selling."

I began to apply these lessons when I joined the private sector. Being a chief executive of a 5,600-employee public agency and advising organization leaders from companies and agencies ranging from 10 to 15,000 employees presented major challenges. For example, suggesting to a CEO of a large law firm that their organizational structure was inhibiting his ability to make sound decisions was a tough sell. I was questioned and challenged at every turn and did not realize that their composition was so entrenched. It took dozens of individual meetings with impacted leaders to show values for them. I was therefore delighted to hear from their COO 2 years later that our recommendations were 92% implemented.

From then on, I crafted my pitch meetings much more carefully, and the 50 speeches I was doing annually for several years focused on problem-solving and benefits. These and many other lessons are incorporated into this book to make your transition from building the product/service to successfully selling it.

Written with humor to make the lessons more memorable and productive, *The Revenue Accelerator* includes tested, savvy strategies and tactics to help you:

- Ease the transition from building a new product/service to selling it
- Access our simplified tools leading to successful sales
- Use our Accelerator Funnel, a visual tool to build and track prospects and customers/clients to uncomplicate your sales efforts
- Apply "real world" approaches that work while also illustrating issues that typically fail

One of my lifetime friends, Steven Venokur, founded and sold the highly successful People Sciences Company. He identifies those who don't know how or when to stop working on their projects and work on the business as "Naked Entrepreneurs" or "Garage Entrepreneurs." This is the primary focus of our book, explaining to start-ups that while working on their product or service, they must also begin to think about how they will finance, market, and sell it. It is these latter steps that move your focus from entirely concentrating on your development in business requirements that will help you succeed.

Along with my own extensive experience of 12 years working as a mentor for the South Bay Entrepreneurial Center in Torrance, California, teaching marketing at California State University Dominguez Hills, and advising the University's Innovation Incubator, I weave Steven's unique understanding of this entrepreneurial group as well as many other successful entrepreneurs' experiences throughout.

Both Steven and I agree with the type of observation made by David Ochi, executive director of the Innovation Incubator, that it is a major mistake to not look at the marketplace before figuring out your product or service. Only then can you build it, finance it, market it, and sell it.

You also need to recognize that, according to the *2020 National Report on Early-Stage Entrepreneurship in the United States,* the "early survival rate" of start-ups between 2012 and 2020 averaged only 20%. Put in other terms, approximately 80% of start-ups fail. In my experience, failures usually occur due to a lack of knowledge and access to resources.

Steve defines an entrepreneur as one who "undertakes new business, develops new products in new and untried areas where the risk is high and outcome unproven." Therefore our 21 Accelerators contain 4 unique features, applying the lessons in real-world, contemporary settings.

The first includes case studies of ongoing start-ups where you can observe many of the accelerator tools in action. Two of the case studies involve my publisher, Made for Success, and me. We want you to see firsthand and in real-time the resourcefulness, initiative, and problem-solving skills you'll need to succeed.

The second novel feature includes quotes from executives, business leaders, and marketing directors converted to cartoons to build retention through humor.

The third is the inclusion of Accelerator Checklists at the end of each chapter. These are designed to enhance retention and provide immediate application opportunities.

And finally, this book contains interviews and comments from more than two dozen start-up entrepreneurs.

Ryan Blaney of Bolimini U.S., a good friend and colleague, described his start-up journey to me this way: "I got unstuck almost [five] years ago, and it feels great. Challenging at times, yes. Stressful at times, sure. But truly doing what makes you happy in life has no salary and no limits."

Let me conclude with a quote from Mary Barra, CEO and president of General Motors:

> **❝People will do the what, if they understand the why.❞**

Our 21 Accelerators will not only show you the *why*, but the *how*.

I am now your acceleration coach, and I'm with you all the way.

THE ACCELERATOR FUNNEL

THE ACCELERATOR FUNNEL is a resource which I reference throughout the book, pictured in Chapter 15. To maximize the revenue growth of your start-up, I recommend you print this now and keep it as a practical resource while you read the book. I encourage you to write in ideas on your own copy of the Accelerator Funnel to kickstart revenue growth.

SCAN ME

ACCELERATOR 1

Make Your Brand Your Takeaway

W E'LL BEGIN WITH an overall view of our sales accelerator system. You will need to lay the foundation for your new business venture with the creation of a unique brand—and then learn to use that brand to its maximum effectiveness.

Wingtips on the Beach

In 1990, as my partners and I were beginning to accelerate the growth of our new consulting company, DecisionQuest, our marketing, business development, and sales were going through a rapid series of changes. Helping our team learn to use the internet and navigate early social media is where my new friend and future mentor, Larry Smith, senior vice president of Levick Communications, came in. We scheduled a pitch meeting for Larry and Richard Levick to meet our COO, Phil, and me at a beach location in Newport Beach, where we were holding a two-day staff session.

Phil and I were sitting on the beach, working on a table with four chairs. At the appropriate time, here came Larry and Richard in their suits, ties, and wingtip shoes across the sand. Their willingness to go the extra mile to meet with us in this most unusual location spoke volumes and told us this would be a great relationship. Needless to say, they had the sale closed by the time they reached our table!

In the years to come, Larry and his team helped us grow, expand, communicate, and sell. To be truthful, Richard, Larry, and I would often meet at New York City and Washington, D.C. steakhouses to hold our review sessions. When I started my own company in 2006, Larry was still mentoring me in my new endeavor.

My unique first prospect meeting with Larry illustrates how many experienced salespeople endeavor to present their brand. They might describe their "brand" as the following:

- "The *'essence'* of your business," according to Mickey Marraffino, managing partner of her firm, MM Marketing.

- "A *'feeling'* associated with the person and their product/service," according to Bryan Heathman, publisher of Made for Success and author of six *Wall Street Journal* best-selling business books.

In my story above, both the essence and feeling of the Levick brand were absolutely clear. They would cross deserts for us to find success. Even better, it was not only an immediate feeling; Indeed, it has continued to this very day.

Your brand is both your takeaway and your differentiator and presents your values.

> "Your brand is what stays in the room after you leave the room."
> —*Jeff Bezos*

Are You Kleenex or Tissue?

Successful selling requires a careful analysis of what people buy and how you present yourself to them. You must directly address how your brand fits with your prospecting—are you known as one of the best or just one of the others? In other words, are you Kleenex or tissue? Are you Xerox or just a copier?

How can you get others to notice what you're selling? By clarifying their needs and issues and discussing how your product or service is a good fit, you should have prospects ready for the next step, **converting their needs to your values**. First, identify someone's need; then, you can offer the value.

When you ask a well-prepared question to determine their need, and they answer it, your response should be, "Here's how we met that need in a similar situation. Would this work for you?" Most likely, they'll say "yes" and see your value. In meeting their need, you are defining your brand for them.

What else have you just done? You have converted their need to one of your values. Follow that process two or three times, especially with somebody who's relatively new to your service or product, and you now have values in their minds that are yours—their "takeaway" from you.

Let me give you a unique example from history of someone who was able to convert his company's values. Think about this: Henry Ford built the first automobile. How did he convert people to leave a horse and get into a car? How did he convince people to give up oats and hay and buy gasoline?

Initially, Ford focused on making the Model T a status symbol. Then, by building an assembly plant capable of turning out a large number of cars, car ownership soon became available for many more people.

Remember this story because it will keep in your mind the importance of selling your values, defined by your brand, and converting their needs. With this story, also remember the following IBM quote that solidifies this whole discussion:

❝Sell what they need, not what you have.❞

Let's restate this slightly. Don't sell what you have; sell what they need. When you do that, you have brought them back around to your values.

Develop Your Brand Using These Five Keys

1. What are the **benefits** you are offering to your clients, to your prospects, to your companies? Keep in mind that they're looking for benefits, both from an individual point of view and from a company's or a service agency's point of view.

2. Are you really offering **solutions** to problems or issues or concerns that they have, and are these solutions also contributing to possible opportunities that they see in their own market?

3. Part of this **conversion process** is talking about results that you've achieved elsewhere. As they explain their needs in more detail, you will need to address them specifically, not just by comparing them to what you've done before.

4. Building **trust** is absolutely critical and is done through references, examples, the professionalism that you present during a meeting or Zoom call, in emails, or wherever the opportunity presents.

5. You are, overall, **presenting the values** that are encompassed in your brand. Those are the values that will stick with these people as they consider purchasing your offerings—the takeaway.

Remember, with every opportunity you need to include these five values... and let me remind you about the IBM quote. "Do not sell what you have... Sell what they need." Sell your brand.

Beware of Leaving an "Anti-Brand"

One major asset you have is your "takeaway." It is an adaption of your brand, focused specifically on the prospect or client you are addressing. No matter what else people remember or don't remember from your meeting or conversation with them, they must take away this core message.

It's important to leave a strong first impression that you can solve their problem. By not being direct and demonstrating how you have solutions for the prospect's problems, you might inadvertently leave an "anti-brand" and waste your preparation and effort.

Remember that old joke, "How do I get to Carnegie Hall?" The answer is, "Practice, practice, practice." One recommendation we always make to our clients is to practice lunch. It is not a throwaway line. If you are meeting for lunch, practice lunch.

Do not walk into a meeting cold. Practice your agenda, key points, and takeaway message with one of your colleagues. The takeaway is the differentiator for you and your firm from your competitors. The wording can have slight differences, but do mention it often during your discussions.

Warren Buffett, CEO of Berkshire Hathaway, has said it best: "It takes 20 years to build a reputation and only 5 minutes to ruin it. If you think about that, you'll do things differently." Even at the earliest stages of developing your new product or service, build positive relationships wherever and whenever you can. Test your brand, your takeaway, your differentiator.

Remember, a brand is not a logo; it is not an isolated image. It is the feeling or the essence of what you are producing that will ultimately resonate with future buyers.

As you progress into the marketing phase, and ultimately into sales, your brand becomes more critical. Creating a brand will first require developing the following:

- A style guide
- A color guide
- Fonts

Once developed, these then lead to the creation of:

- A logo
- A tagline

You Are the Brand to the Customer

Scott Hogle, in his book *Persuade: The 7 Empowering Laws of the SalesMaker,* illustrates this accelerator's most critical message on branding with the following quote:

"How you handle the relationship with the customer is what will create your reputation with them and make the decision as to whether they buy from you again or turn to another company. You are the brand to the customer, not your company."[1]

Once you have your brand, protect it as if your company's life depends on it, because it does.

Accelerator 1 Checklist

Ask yourself the following questions in order to build your company's desired brand:

1. What do people buy?
2. How do you convert their needs to your values?
3. What benefits do you provide?
4. What solutions do you offer?
5. Identify your best results.
6. How are you building trust?
7. Remember, "Sell what they need, not _____."
8. Finally, define your brand.

Looking Ahead to Accelerator 2: Enhance the Customer's Value

Once your brand is established, you will next need a more detailed understanding of your customer's needs in order to bring them value.

ACCELERATOR

Enhance the Customer's Value

UNTIL YOU WALK a mile in your prospects' shoes, you will not know how to bring value to them. What are the most effective steps you can take to get to know them well? Do your research and, in meetings, ask questions focused on what solutions they are seeking and how your product or service provides the solutions and benefits.

Bringing **value** to your prospects may be the only thing they ultimately care about. Once you have learned all you can about them and understand their needs, your goal will be to convert their needs to your values.

By you demonstrating how you have solved their types of problems with others and how these solutions benefited your clients or customers, prospects begin to accept your values. As such, your values now become their values.

❝The very expectation of value creates a dynamic that's optimally conducive to closing.❞

I learned this lesson later in my career when starting my own company, The Closers Group, assisting clients in growing and accelerating revenue. Noting that Xerox corporation found an 87% increase in new business sales with coaching, I offered business development/sales coaching that featured our clients' success rates.

Since my targeted prospect base organizations rarely had formal sales training, my colleagues and I developed and tested a simple, visual system to track follow-up and next steps needed. In fact, they used every other term they could find so as not to use (that horrible word) "sales." The lack of formal sales training had created a void and served to highlight a need that my company could help with.

Our clients' accomplishments confirmed the value of the Xerox analysis. Our 6-month Business Growers (BGers) groups averaged a 65% increase in new business sales. Our 12-month Business Growers groups averaged over a 200% increase in new business sales. These were individuals designated by firm management to participate in our advisory and follow-on sessions. Building their "books of business" was critical to advancing their positions.

By combining tactical, not theoretical, training with ongoing activist coaching, they continued to succeed.

To Kiss a Frog or Not

In an old Brothers Grimm fairy tale, *The Frog Prince*, a princess had to kiss a frog to find her prince. The same can be true in the business of sales. Often in selling, making sure you are dealing with the real decision-maker is critical to closing the sale.

But to understand a business's real values, you'll need to get inside it to recognize who actually makes the decisions. Ask yourself if the business has **hidden decision-makers**. This can be especially difficult to determine at large chains and retail organizations.

If you are selling a food product, for example, and are heading to Walmart, be prepared to go through 100 "Mr. Wonderfuls" (think of *Shark Tank,* where "Mr. Wonderful," Kevin Harrington, asks the toughest questions and provides insight into a company's possible future). Meanwhile, at Trader Joe's, if you go to the head of a whole state, you will be referred back down to the head of a region, who will then tell you to see the individual store manager. You'll need to see if she will buy your product first.

While these may be exaggerations, understand that very often in organizations, there is a final decision-maker on an acquisition, purchase, and the like, and that person will vary depending on the hierarchal structure of the company. Your job is to find out who that person is.

Another factor you need to understand in selling your product or service is the difference between personal buyers or business/company buyers. Personal buyers are focused on delivering your product or service directly to a consumer. These are the purchasing agents and regional managers of large chains who buy products to sell directly to consumers. Those ultimate consumers are most concerned in their selection process with the following considerations:

- Economic Needs
- Psychological Variables
- Social Influences
- Culture and Ethnicity
- Their Purchase Situation

All these factors weigh into their making the decision to purchase or not.

Company/business buyers, on the other hand, evaluate you and your product or service on a much more detailed scale. You will face far fewer buyers who are typically purchasing agents, very aware of legal, governmental, and ethical issues, and using formal purchasing methods.

KTB: Know Their Business

You and your team need to know your prospect's business inside and out. Use the following five keys when asking them questions. Remember that your goal is to convert their needs to your values.

1. **Know who their competitors are.** What is the level of competition your prospect's business faces? Which company is the leader in their industry? Does your prospect's business have particular services or products that are better than the others? You have to familiarize yourself with the whole scope of their competitive field.

2. **Ask if they have new products or services in development.** What is going on in their industry? Has a competitor of theirs introduced something that may become a winner? Do they have something similar in development? When you are looking for their needs, make sure you know what is in development.

3. **Consider internal pressures.** Is the person you are dealing with being pushed out? Are they being given unreachable sales goals or salary caps that can't be met? If so, can you in any way help strategize with them? Can you introduce them to a client/customer of yours in a similar position in a non-competitive business where they can begin to chat about solving problems each faces? What are their personal goals?

Are they looking to grow into another position at another company? Can you serve as a reference? If they trust you, it helps you generate new business and continues a relationship. This is a personal value creator as well.

4. **Deal with bumps in the road.** Always be prepared to deal with bumps in the road. Not too long ago, I was in a client's office when I heard a man scream, yes, scream, from down the hall. His footsteps came pounding to where I was sitting. His face was puffed out and red. "I just lost my biggest client, who was worth about $10,000,000 per year!" he hollered. That company had been acquired, and the man's client had been instructed to terminate all outside relationships within 30 days.

   When I asked him what he planned to do, he responded that he had no idea. He admitted to not having built any other relationships for the past 10 years. He and his team were so involved in delivering the services to this one "super client" that they never took time to build relationships with other companies and agencies.

   "Get on the phone," I told him. His response was, "If I make three calls a day, I'll be done in a week." His predicament clearly demonstrated he didn't comprehend the real business world. Takeovers happen, customers and clients move to new organizations, and downsizing can eliminate long-term contacts. But his lack of leadership in encouraging his team to build new relationships, attend industry meetings and conferences, and meet new prospects was his primary error.

5. **ABR: Always build relationships.** You will continue to see the importance of this concept throughout the book. Build this goal into discussions with your sales teams. You will learn more unusual tactics to build relationships as we continue to emphasize this crucial key for revenue acceleration.

One Size Does Not Fit All

CX, or client experience, provides marketers like you embarking on pitch meetings with a deeper understanding of the value you need to present. As a sales professional, you need to give significant attention to your client/customer's experiences with you in order to understand their needs.

One size never fits all. You should tailor sales according to your client's personality, generation (one of four), and need. What works for one may not work for another.

When you are dealing with multiple clients or customers, it is critical to remain current with each of them. Use the following set of questions for regularly scheduled internal reviews to make sure you have not overextended your ability to continue the highest values for your clients' experiences. Answering these questions will help you refine your value:

- What kind of commitments does the buyer expect you and your firm/company to make?
- What are the buyer's expectations in terms of a rate structure?
- What are the expectations about winning versus settling: completing the deal or letting it go?
- What are the buyer's needs arrayed across a broad spectrum of potential uses?
- Why has a competitor bested you?
- Have you customized your approach, remembering that "one size does not fit all"?

By asking and researching these questions yourself, and hopefully obtaining industry and specific business-related information for your prospect, you will be taking advantage of the latest but overdue method of growing new business—CX. By considering your customer's total experience, your value will be acknowledged and accepted.

Become a Business Partner With Your Customer/Client

Nothing proves more "valuable" than having your customer or client consider you a business partner. The rapidly changing, post-COVID business world indicates that buyers are open to alternatives—working with smaller companies, agencies, and consultancies while identifying new products and services. In the several networking groups I participate in, there have been multiple cross-selling and referral combinations among the member companies.

In order to benefit from this newfound interest in other suppliers and services, have your marketing strategy ready to go. Keep costs or fees palatable. Be accessible and respond quickly. Look for new ideas and ways of highlighting the value you bring to their tables.

Be a business partner to your customers/clients by having the same goals they do—it's called *value*.

Accelerator 2 Checklist

1. Do your clients face internal pressures?
2. Can you anticipate their needs?
3. What are their personal goals?
4. What is their level of competition?
5. What new products or services are in development?
6. Are you ready to deal with the unexpected?
7. ABR = _____.
8. The value I bring is _____.

Case Studies: Introduction

One unique aspect this book offers is having you track along with three colleagues and myself in the real-time formation, development, launching, and progress of an actual start-up business. Our product is now called *Growthbook*. You will find these seven case study pullouts placed throughout *The Revenue Accelerator*:

- The Educational Need
- The Concept and Initial Positioning
- Backend Functionality
- Product Development and Standard Operating Procedures (SOPs)
- Interim Decisions

- Facing the Unknown
- Catapult Into Sales

These case studies provide an inside view as to how we used untapped ingredients from assembly to sales. In addition, we have included more resources you can use in your own start-up.

Case Study #1
The Educational Need

Spending the past 11 years as a volunteer mentor and advisor at the South Bay Entrepreneurial Center in Torrance, California, I gained more understanding of the needs and assistance new entrepreneurs require with their start-ups. Starting my first new company in 2006, The Closers Group, provided me with the same challenges, obstacles, and opportunities others face. As a professor of marketing at California State University Dominguez Hills, I became aware that a number of students wanted to take product ideas and develop them into saleable items. However, no entrepreneurial classes were available, a surprisingly common problem at many American universities.

In October 2019, Professor Michael Grimshaw of California State University Dominguez Hills conducted a review of alumni information from 50 colleges and universities and presented his findings to a College of Business Administration and Public Policy faculty meeting. His team found that over 20% of business students move into a post-graduation role that includes vital sales responsibilities. Therefore, one would expect sales to be a cornerstone discipline of business education. Students are taught fundamentals like preparing marketing plans, forecasting revenue, or reading financial statements. But how effective can these be without an understanding of how to sell?

The need for a sales education tool was obvious. Focusing first on California State University Dominguez Hills students, we needed to address practical skills that would positively change their future businesses. Underrepresented minorities make up 87.5% of CSUDH's student population; 64% are first-generation college students; 69% are Pell Grant eligible; and 48% are all three. Adding sales skills in an entrepreneurial context to their education would provide them improved opportunities to enter the workforce or launch their businesses with confidence.

This same need exists on college campuses throughout the U.S., Canada, and several other countries. The vast majority of undergraduate business and MBA programs no longer offer courses specifically intended to hone the art of sales.

The individuals who are mastering a sales discipline are more than likely not learning it from their college professors; instead, they have turned to the vast world of resources on the internet to bolster their abilities.

Recognizing a hole in the sales education gap, our team set out to create an audio course solution to empower undergrads and MBA students with the tools they needed to holistically understand the sales process. Armed with this understanding, they would be able to positively change their businesses and professional lives.

This added curriculum will help support CSUDH President Parham's stated goal of being "a model for a major urban university."

Looking Ahead to Accelerator 3:
ABR: Always Build Relationships

Be ready for those bumps in the road, for they will surely come along. Do not assume you will always be a winner. Keep working to maintain the relationships.

Customer Lifetime Value, which comes directly from building and continuing relationships, recognizes the economic value of client retention. It represents long-term thinking and is a key element of long-term revenue creation.

ACCELERATOR 3

ABR: Always Build Relationships

A CLIENT OF MINE with over 15 years of business experience saw in an industry journal that an old friend was promoted to the head of a major department at a Fortune 500 company. Although they had gone to ballgames together and taken their kids on playdates, they had inadvertently dropped out of touch during the previous four years. He asked me how to congratulate this friend after so many years.

"Simple," I said, "just pick up the phone and call. Tell him that it has been far too long, but when you saw the promotion announcement, you just had to call and hoped you could get together for lunch." A week later, his friend emailed back saying he was glad to hear from him but was in a major mediation that would take several more weeks. He'd be back in touch.

Later they had lunch and got the families back together again. From that meet-up, my client was introduced to several other senior executives at the company, and new engagements followed. A simple act of reaching out to an old friend yielded an ongoing revenue growth stream for my client.

> **"Direct communication is the best way to create relationships."**
>
> —Jada Pinkett Smith

Another client of mine was struggling with the crashing real estate and financing market several years ago. After discussing his options with me, he agreed that staying in touch with his past customers and contacts would bring a long-term benefit.

So instead of sitting on his hands and waiting for the phone to ring, he committed to staying visible to both his past customers and prospective targets. He set lunches and meetings and updated briefings because he wanted to make sure that when things did turn around, he would be at the top of his clients' minds. This same approach to building relationships has also been successful during and post-COVID.

Keep in mind that being noticed does not always require a big show. Rather, it is often the little things—a written note instead of a text, a face-to-face meeting (Zoom or in-person), or sending a copy of a recent news story that would be of interest that might impact their company.

Staying in touch may not seem like it's going to pay off, but it does. After 6 years of reaching out to a prospect, one of my clients was finally invited to speak at a national organization's annual conference, addressing more than 1,000 attendees. Persistence does pay off—and it can for you, too.

Stay connected, and sales opportunities will abound.

The Myth About Client Retention

Do not believe the old myth that once you have been retained by a customer/client, business generation ceases.

Nothing could be further from the truth. With 50% of your new business every year needing to come from clients, referrals, and prospects, continuing to maintain relationships yields client retention. When I survey a business's customers, two of the top complaints I receive are a lack of communication and being left out of the loop. These comments indicate that you can lose a client after being retained.

When was the last time you asked a client about their present needs? Most likely, their needs have changed since your last conversation with them.

Customer Lifetime Value (CLV) is a concept that recognizes the economic value that client retention brings to a company/ firm/agency. It represents long-term thinking and is a key element of long-term revenue creation.

As the "myth" above is invalid, you need to understand that customers/clients sometimes do leave long-term relationships. You must make sure something does not happen to shatter the relationships you have been building.

Jay Abraham, an internationally known marketing guru, points out three primary reasons why clients leave in his book *Getting Everything You Can Out of All You've Got*:

- Lack of contact leads to their forgetting about the relationship.
- Their situation changes.
- They become dissatisfied.[2]

Clearly, the first of these is easy to overcome. We encourage the companies we work with to develop and take advantage of a contact system. Your customers/clients won't forget about you when you do stay in touch. Let them know what you and your company are currently engaged in, send them an article or reviews that they may be interested in, or ask them to join you on a conference panel, as examples.

Make sure you are communicating the status and next steps of your work on a regular basis and stay on top of changes your clients/customers are experiencing as well. Ask about the challenges they are facing and offer assistance. Be aware of the status of your relationships and be on the lookout for subtle changes in them.

While client dissatisfaction is never comfortable to deal with, it is something you should be cognizant of long before a client disengages. You should pay attention to potential problems right away, even if they seem insignificant, such as small issues arising during an engagement.

Deal with them immediately. Take action and win the client back. Jay Abraham believes that 80 percent of those relationships can be recovered with instant actions—in fact, you may find that by recapturing lost customers/clients, they later become your best clients/customers.[3]

Nine Clues to Knowing Thy Client

Close communications during any client contact effort, whether pursuing new business or arranging for an in-house presentation, are critical to assessing success, analyzing and adjusting to challenges, and continually moving.

You and your colleagues should ask yourselves and answer the following questions before you begin to pursue current, recent, or prospective clients.

1. Who is the decision-maker?
2. What other firms/companies are they using now?
3. When was the last time they hired a new firm or purchased a new product?
4. Do they prefer to communicate by phone or email?
5. What have you done recently to build the relationship?
6. Have you asked ahead of time who else will be attending the meeting?

7. Do you offer periodic review meetings regarding budgets, billing, timeliness of engagement process, and report format?
8. Do you know their pain?
9. How will financial decisions be made?

Another clever way to build relationships is to introduce your clients/customers to your company's other clients who are non-competitive with them. Ask your clients to introduce you to their suppliers, supporters, advisors, and the individuals they use as experts.

In other words, in order to meet new prospects and develop new relationships, work with your customers to "host" meetings with those non-competing and complementary prospects. This is called the Host-Beneficiary Approach.

If you have indeed become their trusted advisor and have established the goodwill that comes from a successful business relationship, they will return the favor when you ask for referrals by introducing you to others. The goodwill and solid relationships that you have will work in your favor.

Relationship Killers

You can find many more positive tactics that help build and keep relationships in the "Kick-Ass Revenue Signals" section of Accelerator 14.

But just as important, if not even more vital, is realizing *what did not work*. Just as we covered above a few of the best ways to build relationships, let's take a quick look at three relationship killers.

1. Don't sell what they already have. Avoid offering to manage and handle what they already have the skills and experience in.

2. Believing that just good results will continue building the relationship is often problematic. It is important to remind them of "their" successes and offer to strategize on future opportunities.
3. Avoid sending too many people to a meeting or on a Zoom call. A smart client/customer will be very aware of the costs of your product or service, add up the expenses of "all those people," and begin to question your real value.

Remember that 50% of your new business every year should be coming from clients, referrals, and prospects—50%! You already know the clients and referrals, so keep up with them, and these sources will continue to expand. As you meet and get to know new prospects, even those who don't buy from you immediately will remain future sources of business.

These relationships are the best sources of your revenue growth.

Looking Ahead to Accelerator 4: Beat the Bumps Along the Way

Even the best of relationships will have disruptions along the way. You cannot anticipate every challenge, but having the right tools to handle these disruptions is key to maintaining successful relationships.

ACCELERATOR 4

Beat the Bumps Along the Way

YOU AND YOUR team will experience bumps along the way. You can't anticipate, as much as we would all like to, the things that will not go smoothly. These **bumps along the way** provide a chance to evaluate what is not working, what is not effective, and what could be done differently.

I would suggest holding "post-mortems" with the team—to not only view problems but "bumps" causing opportunities. Discuss both pitches that worked and those that didn't. How can you turn these opportunity "bumps" into profits?

International marketing guru Jay Abraham includes ideas on how to deal with unexpected bumps in his aforementioned book *Getting Everything You Can Out of All You've Got*. He deserves credit for the following reminders on how to respond to them. Here are a few brief examples found in his book:

1. **Deal with underperforming systems**. Abraham cites a tool the late Peter Drucker, a management consultant, educator, and author, termed "creative abandonment." First, look inside your organization

before you go out on the hunt. Are there tactics or systems that you built in that are not producing leads or generating opportunities? Either reactivate them, refresh them, or stop them. You cannot worry about them when you and the team are "out" there.

2. **Don't miss often overlooked opportunities**. Find a fresh perspective by approaching an acquaintance from a non-competing business and suggesting marketing together (for more detail on this approach, visit Accelerator 17). Perhaps promoting different but complementary products or services together will generate more attention for both of you, especially since you both know a lot of the same people. Put together some lunches. Write an article together. Go and speak to local businesses or at a university program. Create those opportunities. They are out there just waiting.

3. **Identify underutilized assets**. A firm we once worked with had a major problem. Their revenue stream had remained absolutely flat for three years in a row, and they could not understand why. In looking more closely, we saw that they had a huge number of really small engagements, which took a lot of time. However, they also had large engagements that were very profitable, but the firm did not have the staff or the time to deliver the work.

   We helped them make a Drucker review, a "creative abandonment." Their solution was to transfer their smaller clients over a period of time to other organizations who could do the work equally well. This provided the opening to expand those larger assets. Lo and behold, their revenues began climbing 5, 10, even 14% a year.[4]

Reviewing underperforming systems, overlooked opportunities, and underutilized assets helps identify tools that are not being used at all or not being used effectively.

Keep these in mind while using everything you have to overcome those bumps along the way.

Accelerator 4 Checklist #1

1. What are you not using or doing ineffectively?
2. Are you getting everything you can out of all you've got?
3. Do you have underperforming assets?
4. Have you identified overlooked opportunities?
5. Where are your undervalued relationships?
6. How many underutilized collaborative opportunities are there?
7. Can you overcome slip-ups in accountability?

There Are No Guarantees

In life and in business dealings, there are no guarantees. In my role as a business accelerator advisor, I'm often asked about the likelihood of success for various sales approaches. Rather than offering a definitive answer, I often draw on Jay Abraham's responses to hypotheticals.

- Will everything work out as well as we expect it to? Hardly.
- Will some of the things we hope for not happen or turn out worse than we expect them to? Undoubtedly.
- Will there be some things that turn out better than expected? Probably.
- Will you uncover more opportunities as things progress? Yes, if you pay attention.[5]

Make sure you're getting everything you can from all you've got, as Jay Abraham's book title suggests.

After hearing responses to the above questions, I typically ask:

> ## 66 Will you do everything in your power to make the result of this business opportunity an outstanding success? 99

To me, the correct response is "Absolutely!" I want to hear a real commitment. Marketing and selling are no different than any other support service or task. Put the effort in. Then work, work, work until you see the results.

As future Football Hall of Fame quarterback Tom Brady recently said to first-year quarterback Matt Jones:

> ## 66 Keep your head up and keep working. 99
> —Tom Brady

Losing Never Feels Good

If you have ever lost a pitch, an RFP (request for proposal) competition, or a new client/customer, you know it never feels good. When this happens, you might ask yourself a number of questions. Here are three you should consider immediately:

1. Where did your closing skills miss the mark?
2. Did the prospects feel you had a complete understanding of their needs?

3. What is your company/firm lacking that the prospects believe others might deliver?

What? Only 3% Are Ready To Buy?

What 3%? Where did 3% come from? Is it made out of thin air? How is it relevant?

In their book *Business Breakthroughs*, Tony Robbins and Chet Holmes present research that shows only **3% of all your contacts are actually ready to buy**—that's right, 3%.

Some 7% are willing to listen if you stay in contact with them. An additional 30% might be interested if you let them know and remind them you have something to offer. Another 30% aren't even thinking about what you are doing. The remaining 30% are "out to lunch," basically not thinking at all. They are just performing their regular tasks and not considering anything else.[6]

Now go back to your 3%. Focus on them. That is where you build the start with customers you know and referrals you have. In the beginning, focus on finding quick wins. Help anyone working with you on this campaign to do the same thing. Finding wins will make you feel better, encourage your sales team, and stimulate more effort and success.

In our seminars, we emphasize that **a full 50% of your new business every year** should be coming in from clients/customers, referrals, and prospects. This requires extra effort beyond the 3% cited above. Because Chet Holmes and Tony Robbins also propose in their book that it takes an average of **five to eight contacts to land new business**—yes, five to eight![7] As you build your marketing and sales plan, understand the hard work it will take to land that one new client.

There is an old expression:

"If you chase two rabbits, you won't catch either one."

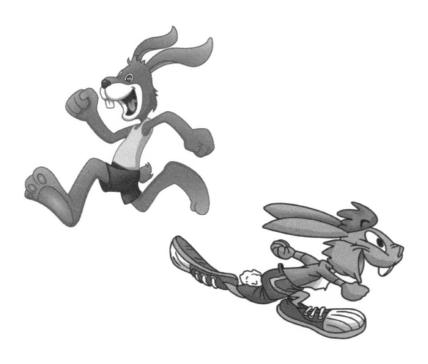

So, focus, focus, focus. Focus on that 50%, get those 5 contacts per customer done, and even try to make it in only 3. Remember that 3% and identify them by building them into your sprint funnel. Do not chase two rabbits.

Accelerator 4 Checklist #2

1. Which prospects do you focus on first?
2. What is the most overlooked factor in sales?
3. What percent of your current prospects are ready to buy?
4. What percent of your current prospects are willing to listen?

5. What percent of your current prospects might be interested?
6. Do you have your team focusing on quick wins?
7. If you chase two rabbits, what will be the result?

Maximizing Rejection

What? Maximize rejection, you say? YES. OK, let's say you have a proposal that was not accepted. Don't just discard their decision. Instead, simply put them on the lower end of your priority list.

Think about it this way. With your client/customer acquisition effort, you have already made the investment of time and money and were close to getting a deal. The person or people you were meeting with have actually done the same thing with their time and investment. They cared enough to meet with you, exchange ideas, perhaps even look at a proposal.

Think about maximizing rejection this way. If you stay in touch with those "nos" on a regular basis, you might ultimately win 10% of them for new business in the future. Additionally, because you have already made the primary investment with them, this revenue will go directly to your **bottom line**, to your company's ROI. For these reasons, you should always keep maximizing any rejection.

According to Nanneke Dinklo, director of marketing for a $100,000,000 brand-packaging company, client/customer acquisition costs are the most often overlooked expenses for a start-up. Don't let your expenses run so high that the bump along the way is to postpone marketing and sales.

What if a prospect's "no" continues? In that case, let's revisit Peter Drucker's concept of creative abandonment. His approach means this: When you have been looking at an effort that is not working, and the cost does not seem worthwhile, make a decision. This is comparable to the earlier underutilized assets discussion.

If something is not producing and looks as though it won't, or you cannot afford to put in the time and energy to fix it, abandon it.

Take that effort, that money, and that time and apply them elsewhere. If you continue to receive "nos," you do not need to stay in touch with every one of those prospects. This is an evaluation you must regularly make as part of your efforts to grow revenue rapidly.

Make sure that you do not spend so much focus on one potential prospect or client that it eats into your available sales time. Abandoning prospects is not an easy decision to make; however, it is sometimes critical to do so.

66Nothing will work unless you do.99

—Maya Angelou

Let's take a look at how you should continue to invest in a prospect. You have already spoken with them, so they know who you are and understand your offering. Assuming the "brand that you left in the room" is a strong one, and your "takeaway" message has resonated, they remain potential future clients/customers. Send them a copy of a relevant article. Invite them to an event. Apply the invisible marketing tactics covered in Accelerator 10.

As we mentioned, when you convert those "nos" into "yesses," the profit from them goes directly to your bottom line. You had already made the initial investment. Therefore, the end result in finally converting them could not be better.

Don't Give Up. Don't Ever Give Up.

Jimmy Valvano was a varsity head basketball coach at Rutgers University. This was his very first varsity head coaching position. Before his first game, he began pacing back and forth outside of the locker room, thinking, "What do I say to inspire my team? What do I do to motivate them?"

He started thinking about Knute Rockne, that famous Notre Dame football coach who always inspired his teams. So, Coach Valvano finally walked into the locker room with his very first varsity team and said, "Go win this one for good old Notre Dame!"

He walked out of the locker room horrified at his mistake. Yet he needed to give the team the incentive to play hard. He walked back in and said, "Don't Give Up. Don't Ever Give Up."

This is the bottom-line message about why maximizing rejection will work for you. Do not put your "nos" in a discard file as they still hold potential for future business. You and your team were actively engaged with the prospect, and they spent the time with you hearing your proposal, getting to start a relationship, and investing their time in the meeting or call.

"If I made three phone calls a day,
I'd run out of clients to call in two weeks!"

My Small Bump and Tropicana's Big Bump in the Night

Looking back on the greater scheme of things, I can recognize one major bump I experienced along the way in my career, one which I actually caused, as a good teaching example here. But painful bumps happen to major corporations as well.

In my case, I made the mistake of leaving a highly successful partnership after 28 years to join a large firm with over 700 professionals and a 500-person support staff. The firm created a new role for me to improve the individual sales efforts of mid-level professionals.

With intensive group and individual coaching, I had already tracked approximately $5,000,000 in sales for my new firm. But it seemed my overhead expenses were too high, like painting an office and ordering discounted furniture to replace pieces that were falling apart. That, at least, was my view. They never gave me termination reasons, just sent me on the way with a payout. It was a tough lesson for me. I had given up something tried and true and successful for a potential opportunity that did not work out. To this day, I still regret making that move.

Now taking a longer-term view, this unwelcome experience forced me to look at the market for my advisory and consulting services, form a new company, and become a start-up entrepreneur. A significant portion of this book comes from those experiences and what I've learned from colleagues and clients.

Another more prominent example of a big "bump" would be the marketing/branding mistake Tropicana orange juice made several years ago. You may recall their logo/brand, a beautiful orange with a straw poking out the top. Someone made the decision to drop it from the packaging, and sales consequently dropped a reported 20% in the first month.

Guess what the decision was to get them off the bumpy road and back on track?

After recognizing that they disrupted their highly recognized brand, Tropicana executives immediately took action. They restored the original packaging and mounted an aggressive marketing campaign to reinforce the brand in all the retail outlets and the media.

Personal bumps along the way may also occur, such as running out of capital. Keeping afloat during the start-up phase of your new business will always be on your mind. Recently I attended my high school reunion (I won't tell you what year!). In exploring what several of my entrepreneurial buddies had to say about their experiences in starting new businesses, the answer was universal...

"I get paid last."

Their stories were similar. In the beginning, all of their revenue went to paying for the supplies, product manufacturing, service descriptions, marketing, and employees. These friends were highly experienced businesspeople and understood the importance of making sure their vendor and supplier relationships received payment for all due invoices. Fortunately, they had personal funds to keep building the product.

If you are a "garage" or "naked" entrepreneur with limited or no access to funding, the worst bump along the way would be an inability to continue the product development due to lack of capital.

A well-thought-out business plan early in the entrepreneurial process will help you recognize the likelihood of problems like these arising. That plan needs to include a client/customer recovery plan. By anticipating that there will be "bumps" and organizing your responses ahead of time, your confidence in marketing and selling will increase.

Accelerator 4 Checklist #3

1. Update that 3% who are willing to buy.
2. Learn how important diversity and inclusion are to your prospects.
3. Begin building metrics to measure and plan for future growth.
4. Continually update the needs of your clients/customers and prospects.
5. Conduct "post-mortems" on every pitch and every proposal.
6. Look closely for "price sensitivities" and who the real decision-makers will be.
7. Practice your pitches, reply to sample questions—and then practice some more.
8. Do a quarterly update to our Action Program Creator, attached in the appendix.

66The secret of getting ahead is getting started. 99
—Mark Twain

Looking Ahead to Accelerator 5: The 15 Must-Have Attributes

As an entrepreneur, the confidence you have in the value your new product or service will bring to those who need it should be shown in your demeanor. By overcoming the "bumps" faced during the development and early marketing phases, the attitude you now convey becomes a key element in sales success.

John Maxwell, in his book *The Difference Maker*, names attitude as one of four key ingredients for successful selling. The other ingredients include relationships, leadership, and equipping people.

ACCELERATOR 5

The Must-Have Attributes
for the Entrepreneur

"YOU NEED TO smile more," I was told by speech coach and communications specialist Susanne Egli from Communication Navigation in Minneapolis. I spent a full day "emoting" to an empty theatre-in-the-round acting out Chaucer and Shakespeare.

She told me to bring in more humor and smile more during seminars, presentations, speeches, and, most importantly, sales pitch meetings.

It was, therefore, a real honor when editor Allard Winternink, in the April 2017 edition of *Legal Business World*, called our marketing coloring book a "hysterical and fun way to teach lawyers business development."

Recently updated through Made for Success Publishing, Inc., our B2B Sales Coloring book includes quotes from sales managers and executives about marketing and sales. We have converted these quotes into cartoons relating directly to overcoming challenges.

To further emphasize the importance of smiling, I would like to add a Harvey Mackay quote found in his book *You Haven't Hit Your Peak Yet!*:

> **❝I learned years ago that one of the most powerful things you can do to have influence with others is to smile at them... Smiles never go up in price or down in value.❞**
>
> —Harvey Mackay

Emails won't and don't . . .

. . . end in handshakes.

Get Close and Personal

You (and your sales team) are continuing in the "go" phase of chasing and aggressively sprinting to obtain new revenue. You need to get "close and personal" in spite of any inhibitors to the contrary. A recent British Airways ad expresses it like this: "Emails Don't End in Handshakes."

Of course, British Airways wanted the readers to jump on their company's planes and spend lots of money. From our perspective, it illustrates the critical need to learn more about your clients and prospects, getting them to feel more comfortable and trust in you and your product or service.

Remember ABR: Always Build Relationships

Consider the following eight tips as you're continuing to strengthen relationships with your current clients and beginning to build relationships with your prospect list.

1. **How do your prospects want to receive information**? Do they want emails? Do they want phone calls? Are they passing on what they receive from you to others in their company who have different disciplines?

2. **How do they want to reach out to you?** If it's by text or email, make sure you and your team are checking text and email regularly. You are selling to four different generations, and you need to know both how to reach each of them and how they want to deal with you.

3. **Deal with problems promptly**. Respond to complaints and fix them quickly. Once you fix the issue, let them know asap that it's been fixed.

4. Use the **invisible marketing tool,** which looks to draw a prospect or customer in to assist you in a way that compliments them. For example, send them a draft of an article you are writing and ask for comments. By

doing this, you are demonstrating that you trust and value them.

Then, when you have future calls with the client/ customer, add, "When you had that problem and we fixed it immediately—is it still going OK?" In asking that, what have you done here? It's simple; you asked them to remember your prompt attention and service.

This is also an important part of your **listening** tools. It reminds them of a handshake.

5. **Refer business to their clients and customers.** Hold "beyond emails" frequent discussions, reminding them where you are in their services or product delivery. Ask if any of their customers or prospects need what you are offering/providing them. If so, follow up by inquiring if they could arrange introductions for you.

6. **Introduce them to your clients and customers.** You know how important referrals are to you and your team. By helping them build their business, this is another way to build trust.

7. **Utilize business associations, both yours and your prospects.** Invite your clients to your meetings and ask to go to theirs.

At your associations, be very gracious about introducing them to others who could help with their businesses. If there is an interesting speaker at your meeting, invite them. If there is an interesting speaker at one of their upcoming associations, ask if you can attend. If you have sponsored a table at a major fundraiser, invite them and some of their other staff.

These and many other tactics and techniques really help you and your team get to know the clients and prospects and for them to know and trust you. We cannot say it enough: Keep on building relationships.

Reach out for that handshake and smile!

❝It's not the school prom.❞

—Robert Herjavec of Shark Tank

This quote illustrates that a unique group of attributes is necessary to sell your product or service successfully. Entrepreneurship is certainly not a dance filled with music, beautifully dressed people, and no cares in the world. If you are proceeding as a "naked entrepreneur," building your service or product in a "garage," you must do more than pay the bills.

One of my oldest and dearest friends, Steve Venokur, founded a company called People Sciences.

Steve started a couple of companies but had the good fortune of selling People Sciences to SAP for a notable amount of money. In a recent conversation with me, he noted the competencies most critical to successful product development and market acceptance.

He coined the phrase "**naked entrepreneur,**" describing a person who begins their business with nothing but an idea and builds the product/service on their very own. Naked entrepreneurs often have so many concerns hitting them at once that they just don't know how to begin.

15 Attributes the Naked Entrepreneur Must Possess

All naked entrepreneurs who win in the end exhibit a combination of common attributes. Most often, beginning with nothing more than an idea and ending up with a successful business is a tough path. Although the following is perhaps not an exhaustive list, here are 15 must-have attributes for the naked entrepreneur, presented in random order:

1. **Self-reliance,** the confidence to continue forward when the going gets tough, like losing financing or staff.
2. **Adaptability,** the ability to be nimble, to switch gears rapidly to new approaches, technology, finance, marketing, and sales—all by yourself.
3. **Competence** in your product or service area.
4. **Critical thinking** skills to create value.
5. **Sound decision-making and listening** abilities.
6. **Self-motivation,** including the willingness to take initiative and be persistent. This is also the number-one attribute identified by Yolanda Guibert, chair of two Vistage boards and a colleague of mine at the South Bay Entrepreneurial Center in Torrance, California.[8]
7. **Generator of fresh ideas**, such as always being on the lookout for new approaches.
8. **Demonstrated effective leadership** with peers, project support, and in people management. Consider the "Six Essentials of Leadership" from my book *Lead Like a Boss*, published by Made for Success.[9]
   - Listening
   - Making decisions
   - Communication
   - Accountability
   - Taking minimal risks
   - Legacy
9. **Resourcefulness** in making do with what you've got or finding others to help.
10. **Effective organization,** demonstrated by an adeptness in understanding manufacturing, marketing, sales, and financing.

11. **Overcomer of challenges,** disappointments, upsets, delays, and rejection.
12. **Intuitive grasp of branding.** Will the customer clearly understand my product or service? What should I call it?
13. **A willingness to share the success.** In a recent conversation with me, David Ochi, director of the Innovative Incubator at California State University Dominguez Hills, cited the following story that illustrates this attribute. Years ago, he met a custodian at the Boston Red Sox stadium who was wearing a World Series Championship ring. When Ochi asked him about it, the gentleman said every person who worked for the Red Sox was given a championship ring, every person.
14. **A built-up level of trust.** Trust builds sales. It drives expectations, successful delivery, repeat sales, and referrals. According to a January 2021 PricewaterhouseCoopers survey of small- to medium-sized company CEOs and presidents, the three most important issues for them coming out of the COVID pandemic were these:
    • Performance management
    • Trust
    • Customer relations[10]

Note that all three deal with buyers, customers, and clients. It further supports the importance of attitude.

15. **Possessing high business ethics** is an absolute requirement for successful entrepreneurs. Moral standards should steer your decisions. According to the American Marketing Association Statement of Ethics in 2014, all businesses should hold the following ethical values:
    • Honesty: to be forthright in dealings with customers and stakeholders.

- Responsibility: to accept consequences for their marketing decisions and strategies.
- Fairness: to balance justly the needs of the buyer with the interests of the seller.
- Respect: to acknowledge the basic human dignity of all stakeholders.
- Transparency: to create a spirit of openness in marketing operations.
- Citizenship: to fulfill the economic, legal, philanthropic, and societal responsibilities that serve stakeholders.[11]

> **❝No matter what level you are in your organization, learn how to pack parachutes.❞**
> —Harvey Mackay

10 Attributes of All Entrepreneurs

We have just listed some common attributes naked entrepreneurs specifically need. Valerio Giannini, in a worksheet he wrote for his classes at the University of California Irvine, offers another assessment of additional traits all entrepreneurs need. Note that these involve both temperament and talent.

Consider the descriptions below and ask yourself how well each pertains to you.

1. In school, business, or sports, you tend to fall into team leadership roles.
2. Often not satisfied with the first answer, you tend to dig deeper.

3. The notion of turning your mind on for eight hours during work and then placing it on standby for the rest of the day is foreign to you.
4. You're obsessive, but in a good way. When you have a vision, you get excited and see the endpoint and the general steps to get there.
5. When you start on something, you see it through.
6. You celebrate other people's success. It doesn't upset you or make you jealous.
7. You dislike the word "employee" for subordinates; you'd prefer "team member."
8. When you walk into a store, restaurant, or other business, you think about how you would run it.
9. You started your first business at an early age, perhaps a lemonade stand.
10. "Work" has never felt like effort.

11 Mistakes that Offend Businesspeople

We have spent many years talking with clients and seminar attendees about what offends them in sales meetings. Some of their answers are quite surprising. Ensure that in building positive attitudes, you do not make these mistakes.

1. Offering to manage and handle what they already have the skills to do.
2. Relying on good results but not building the relationship.
3. Using offensive humor during meetings.
4. Buying a table at one of their special charity events and not showing up or sending the wrong people.
5. Sending too many people to a meeting.
6. Choosing the wrong medium to communicate.
7. Surprising the customer/client with late-breaking information.

8. Showing a lack of business etiquette such as using cell phones, taking calls, or bringing the "potted plant" in the room and not engaging.
9. Sending out cold-call materials to them.
10. Not being prepared for a meeting.
11. Not following up with them after client-sponsored events.

Clients and customers mention these complaints to me so often in seminars and one-to-one coaching that they need to be emphasized.

Don't throw trust and validity out the door by sending too many people to a meeting. Ask who else will be there well ahead of time and what kind of information you can provide that would help them in the upcoming meeting. Most importantly, once you find out who will be there from their company, find out about their backgrounds and interests.

Let me emphasize that you never offer a service or product your client/customer/prospect already has. Do offer something new and different you think they might need that you have already discussed ahead of time. Don't just rely on previous positive results.

Make sure to always build the relationship. Remind them frequently of the results you have helped them achieve. Check in with them. Are there other tasks you can assist them with? Is their staff having difficulty understanding what your company is doing for them or how your product works? Let them know you would be happy to explain any problematic areas to them while emphasizing that you enjoy working with them.

Do not tell questionable jokes. Even if you have an established relationship, you never know who else in the room might be offended. Besides, it is not professional. Just don't do it. A related problem could also be members of your team who talk among themselves while in a pitch meeting.

That is *rude*, pure and simple. Your people need to be better trained than that.

Being on cell phones is one of the four or five most frequent complaints I hear. Make it mandatory that before you and your team enter through the door to a meeting that everyone turns their cell phones off, not just silences them. Remind them not to not even look at them. Break that nasty habit.

Getting to know your client includes agreeing in advance on which type of communication they most prefer: email, phone, Zoom, in-person, or maybe even fax. Clarify how they want to receive information and how you will respond. This encoding and decoding is especially critical as you approach prospects and clients from four current generations, each with its own communication preferences.

Do remember business etiquette by saying "thank you," shaking hands, asking questions, and being responsive in a timely fashion. If they stand, you stand. It may seem old-fashioned, but it is not. The people you are talking with will remember every little move they feel is annoying. Remember this Jeff Bezos quote:

"Your brand is what stays in the room after you leave."

By all means, be prepared for the meeting. Practice what will be said. Prepare ahead of time by anticipating the questions they are likely to ask and pre-designate the team member who will respond.

Accelerator 5 Checklist

1. What are six relationship-building tools?
2. Are you ready to deal with complaints?
3. Have you established their preferred methods of communication?
4. Have you referred business to your clients and customers?
5. Do you conduct periodic reviews with your clients?
6. Are you presenting non-business contacts to your customers?
7. Do you attend non-business events you have been invited to?

Case Study #2
Licensing

One option that start-up entrepreneurs can use to finance their start-up is licensing. This gives a third-party rights to sell your product or service with a promise of income for using the licensed content. For example, Disney may license its characters to a company that makes lunch boxes.

When Bryan Heathman began building his publishing business, he was working a day job four days per week. Therefore, he had the fifth day to develop a new business opportunity, which was a spoken-word audio licensing company with content from the most famous speakers on the planet.

Bryan and his business partner approached companies for retail distribution, including Costco and other big-box retailers. One of Costco's vendors, Topics Entertainment, agreed to license, manufacture, and distribute six different information products focusing on leadership, sales, and public speaking skills. Royalties from the sales of these products were paid to the content partners quarterly based on a percentage of the wholesale revenues.

Initially, Costco tested the products in a dozen stores to evaluate the sell-through potential of the products. The volume of sales exceeded the expectations of the Costco buyer. Based on the successful test, the products were rolled out chainwide.

The start-up received added value and numerous benefits from this licensing arrangement. The biggest payback included investing minimal out-of-pocket cash to gain nationwide distribution. Having early cashflow without the massive start-up costs for warehousing, accounting overhead, and manufacturing typical to this sort of business added to the equation. Without the intensive investment, the company could continue working on developing new products and expanding its footprint in a fast-growth marketplace.

Looking Ahead to Accelerator 6: Finance Yourself

Yolanda Guibert, a chair of two Vistage Boards, believes that, all too often, starters are so "gung-ho" on building their new product or service that they don't take time to think through financing and selling.

Also, Don Davis, a highly regarded attorney with 40 years of experience matching producers with financing, also finds that steering start-ups in the right direction, with a dose of reality, is often the difference between their success and failure.

ACCELERATOR 6

Finance Yourself

STARTING MY OWN firm, The Closers Group, was downright scary. For the past 20 years, I have had the good fortune of having 100 fellow employees working together. Now I was on my own—a start-up.

Fortunately, I was beginning with a large group of relationships and savings that allowed me to begin selling and marketing. The first obstacle, which became quite humorous, was seeing the trademark search reveal over 1,500 companies with the name "closer" in them. The law firm helping me form the company sent a phonebook-sized report with companies using the name "closer." Would this mean me having to find a new company name? However, the temporary cloud lifted when I saw they were all garage-door companies and would be in no way competitive with our business development and strategic business planning services.

This accelerator is included for those start-up entrepreneurs who, as my strategic partner Frank Mims V says, "are focused so much on their product that they are not thinking ahead." They ultimately realize they need financing but don't know where to go.

Interviews I've conducted with several entrepreneurs, financiers, and intermediaries have all provided similar answers to this one question:

"What tools do I need when looking for funding?"

Get Your House in Order

Mike Manahan, my colleague teaching at CSU, Dominguez Hills, and in mentoring at the South Bay Entrepreneurial Center, has served as chief financial officer for 3 publicly traded companies, started and owned 7 small businesses, and advised more than 100 management teams. His advice for anyone starting a business is direct and succinct:

"Get your house in order."

He points to eight basic requirements that potential lenders will want to examine:

1. A business plan
2. Financial projections
3. Revenue drivers to acquire customers
4. Capital needs
5. Organization documents (most often overlooked):
   - Established legal corporation
   - Organization minutes
   - Officers
   - Corporate office location
   - Shares/shareholders, if any
   - Taxes, budgeting, and financing costs
6. Trademark protection
7. Contingency plan
8. A track record

Finding The Chocolate Sauce and Whipped Cream

Once your new product or service is in hand, how do you *top it off* with the necessary financing to make it a financial success? Plus, how do you avoid negative consequences in the search for capital—that is, if you can even obtain it?

Valerio Giannini, managing partner of NewCap Partners, Inc., cites the following spectrum of sources for private equity capital. He uses this in one of his entrepreneurial courses at University of California Irvine.

1. Personal sources (family, friends, partners)
2. "Angel Groups" (investment clubs)
3. Seriously high net-worth individuals
4. Private placements with individuals and institutions you don't know
5. Private equity funds (including SBICs)
6. Venture capital funds (VCs)
7. Small Business Administration (SBA) and other governmental sources
8. Small Business Innovation Research (SBIR) grants
9. Economic Injury Disaster Loans (EIDL) or other emergency funds
10. Crowdfunding
11. Strategic corporate investors

Even if you have prepared all the requirements needed, obtaining capital is not easy. Only a small portion of start-ups and new entrepreneurs are able to secure financing.

It is often **intermediaries** who help bring the entrepreneur together with funding sources. Two highly successful intermediaries are Don Davis, an attorney in the Los Angeles area with 40 years of experience, and Gary Spain, president of InterCorp Resources, Intl. When called on for advice,

Don starts new entrepreneurs out with "a dose of reality." Similarly, Gary responds to initial inquiries by telling them, "Make sure your ask is complete."

Both handle start-up financing, something which they acknowledge is extremely difficult to obtain without some type of proven track record. Typically negotiating for and representing medium and large companies in the multimillions range, they look at all of Giannini's 11 sources stated above. They take their responsibilities to assist new entrepreneurs seriously, giving them sound advice.

Beware of the Sharks and Alligators

Michael S. Manahan, a professor of finance at California State Dominguez Hills and former CFO, wrote *Secrets to Raising Capital* (2nd edition), a must-read book for start-up entrepreneurs. In Manahan's own words, he calls the book a "real world guide to help you navigate the tricky waters of raising capital and dealing with the sharks and alligators." The book explains the psychology behind the guys with the money:

- Why they ask the questions they do
- Why they act the way they do
- What motivates them
- How you can increase your chances of getting their attention and their money as they are doing the following:
  - o Reading your business plan
  - o Reviewing your numbers
  - o Listening to your presentation
  - o Considering putting up the money you need for your business

"A lot is going on, and if you don't understand it, your chances of getting the funding become just that more difficult."[12]

While this may sound discouraging to many, it is reality. Mr. Manahan has spent time talking with bankers in New York, venture capitalists in Silicon Valley, high net-worth individuals, factors, and hard-money lenders.

His conclusion—simple accounting does not apply.

Entrepreneurs Make Incredibly Stupid Mistakes

Valerio Giannini has stated, "Entrepreneurs make incredibly stupid mistakes." It is as though they have invested a lot of time and money in development but don't realize they have downsized their product's value. It's like converting dollars to donuts where once you eat the donuts, there is nothing left from your investment.

The following **notable mistakes** are sourced from the same handouts Giannini uses in his entrepreneurial classes:

- Accepting financials that are not specifically audited
- Not asking to see tax returns soon enough
- Trusting earnings when inventories aren't audited

1. Corporate Finance
   - Making a major commitment premised on a tentative future financing
   - Not isolating liabilities of new ventures from another company
   - Not having enough "authorized" shares
   - Not understanding the fine print
   - Neglecting to perfect a security interest immediately

2. Cash Management
   - Holding back payroll withholding taxes for "just a few weeks"

- Not managing accounts payable when short of cash
- Extending more credit than you can afford to lose

3. Undocumented Expenses, Advances, and Loans
   - Charging expenses without supporting details
   - Promising to cover expenses that aren't deductible or equal to income
   - Approving loans to shareholders without formal documentation and interest

Accelerator 6 Checklist

Using the Valerio Giannini list of stupid "mistakes," make note and steer clear to ensure your new product or service is well protected.

Looking Ahead to Accelerator 7: Capital for Minorities and Women

Financing is the one overall need most often overlooked by start-ups during their developmental phase. Understanding where local entrepreneurial support groups are located, major funding sources for women and minorities, and tactics to help work around barriers to financing are all discussed.

ACCELERATOR 7

Capital for Minorities and Women

ACCESS TO CAPITAL for minorities and women was a special focus of the South Bay Economic Institute, the Mervyn M. Dymally African American Political and Economic Institute, and the CSU Dominguez Hills College of Business Administration and Public Policy. They surveyed women entrepreneurs, including specifically African American women entrepreneurs, in Los Angeles's South Bay and the greater Los Angeles area and concluded the following:

- Women entrepreneurs rely more on family, friends, or banks for funding rather than venture capital, private equity, or crowdfunding.
- The majority of women entrepreneurs consider the cost of capital, lack of a network, and financial hardships as the major obstacles facing them.
- African American women entrepreneurs cite barriers such as collateral requirements, cost of debt (high interest rates), lack of a network, financial hardships, and lack of financial support.

Gary Polk is a black businessman, CEO, business consultant, university professor, author, and founder of the Polk Institute of Social Entrepreneurship. He and I have taught at CSU, Dominguez Hills, and originally met when he was the volunteer director of the South Bay Entrepreneurial Center. In a recent interview I conducted with him, he made the following observation: "Capital is given to people who look like the funders." For more discussion on this topic, please see Polk's book *Why Black & Brown Entrepreneurs Fail (To Win)*.

Continuing in a related book, *Why Women Entrepreneurs Fail (To Win)*, Polk mentions obstacles such as a lack of access to capital, absence of a strong network, and work/life balance concerns.[13] Typically, women entrepreneurs are more impacted by these types of concerns.

Dr. Jennifer Brodmann, the co-director of the South Bay Economic Institute and a minority herself, co-authored the above book with Polk. At a recent South Bay Economic annual report meeting, she mentioned the importance of "knowing people who know people."

> **❝Know people that know people.❞**
> —Dr. Jennifer Brodmann,
> CSU Dominguez Hills

Polk and Brodmann both express an overwhelming concern for minority entrepreneurs. Their research shows that many of their fellow minorities need help succeeding in the entrepreneurial world. Their two books offer "… the kind of help that is not always common in our minority communities," according to my conversation with Dr. Brodmann.

Some minority entrepreneurs find creative ways to finance their start-ups. One unique solution two black entrepreneurs in Houston found was finding a professor at the University of Houston's business school who was willing to have his senior-most classes develop business plans and financial projections. The entrepreneurs then used these to obtain the needed funding for their start-ups.

A further observation on the hindrances minorities and women face in funding their start-ups comes from an interview I conducted with Lloyd Johnson, CEO of Black In-House Counsel (BIHC) and Chief Legal Executives. Lloyd and I worked together many years ago when he began Chief Legal Executives. My company at that time, DecisionQuest, helped to sponsor part of their quarterly meetings.

It was Lloyd who, unable to secure the needed capital from traditional sources, found Fortune 100 chief legal officers willing to commit sponsorship funds to get the new organization going. In my interview with him, he did concur with Gary Polk's view about funding for minority start-ups. He shared from his view that you "had to know someone, who knew your background, who believed in you" in order to be even considered for funding.

There is some positive news, however. In 2020, both the Women Entrepreneurship Report and the African American Women Entrepreneurship Report noted that investments for women and minority-owned businesses have increased, with total capital raised from $5,000,000 in 2016 to $35,000,000 in 2019.

The statistics in the Women Entrepreneurship Report also show that women and minorities are actively sourcing funding as follows: finding and working with small business development centers, 35.38%; incubators, 34.38%; co-working spaces, 34.38%; and business accelerators, 28.13%.[14]

Social Entrepreneurship

Your attitude and consideration of social entrepreneurship when building your new product or service is essential to being a contributing member of the world society.

Gary Polk has been a colleague of mine at both the South Bay Entrepreneurial Center in Torrance, California, and as a fellow professor at California State University Dominguez Hills. Starting out as a bank teller, graduating from Loyola Marymount University, gaining a master's from CSUDH, and spending 10 years at the old Bank of America, he has spent many of the last years as an adjunct professor of business management, ethics, and entrepreneurship at CSUDH.

He and fellow professor Mike Manahan founded the Polk Institute for Social Entrepreneurship. It is a notable nonprofit that provides high-level, real-world training and instruction in the area of social entrepreneurship. It is a recognized business model that combines the disciplines of market capitalism with innovative approaches to solving societal problems.

Social entrepreneurs have both a passion for business and a compassion to make a positive impact on the Triple Bottom Line, or the new Three Ps: People, Planet, and Profit.

In considering how your new product or service will benefit a potential market, consideration of these Three Ps may also lead you to a higher recognition factor and special access to designated capital.

The Polk Institute's goal is to expose social entrepreneurship as a viable business option and method to find true financial freedom for 70 percent of their targeted trainees—underrepresented black and brown minorities. Its students are serious about wanting to own a business.

Environmental, Social, and Corporate Governance (ESG)

Environmental, Social, and Corporate Governance (ESG) is a relatively new scoring system applying non-financial factors to measure a business's attention to the environmental and social arenas. ESG is now being used by multiple start-up funding sources. These funding sources evaluate a company's ESG ethical score in addition to the usual financial investment risks to determine their offers of any loans and grants.

Accelerator 7 Checklist

1. What are some tactics to work around barriers to funding?
2. Is your product or service the type that a professional association or business group might support?
3. If your new idea is environmentally friendly, how would it score on the ESG scoring system?
4. Have you identified entrepreneurial support/training groups that can assist and educate you on the tools for success? What are they?

Case Study #3
The Concept and Initial Positioning

By introducing Bryan Heathman, publisher of Made for Success, to David Ochi, executive director of the Innovation Incubator at California State University Dominguez Hills, I was delighted to find an immediate understanding of the problem and options to solve it. Following our initial discussions in Month 1, we have met by Zoom every week to plan and jumpstart the opportunity.

The CSUDH Innovation Incubator has partnered with Made for Success, the owner of one of the world's largest audio libraries of personal development content featuring well-known sales leaders like Zig Ziglar and Tom Hopkins, as well as other up-and-coming ones. The primary focus of our project would be to break the barriers of sales education using proven sales training techniques tailored to start-ups and their unique needs. Our course would include teaching digitally savvy strategies other businesses are using to get ahead. Students would learn the following:

o Sales skills that launch early revenues in start-ups.
o Sales skills that translate well into entry- and mid-level sales roles.
o Establishment of sales management strategies and techniques for scalable growth.

The plan is to include a group of student interns who will work with the *Growthbook* team to build a world-class mobile subscription service that will empower the next generation of start-up leaders. With content from recognized industry experts who have a global reach, both students and community entrepreneurs will gain access to the mindset and skill set needed to launch companies and careers that will have true impact on themselves and their communities.

These eight selling skills would be included:

o Professional development
o Practice management
o Business ethics
o Entrepreneurial skills
o Prospecting
o Sales skills
o Lead generation
o Lead capture

To recognize the effort students will put in when taking the courses, they will earn digital credentials that boost their online credibility.

We agreed on the initial positioning for *Growthbook* as "Sales for start-ups."

Looking Ahead to Accelerator 8: Don't Sell What They Already Have

Your Unique Selling Proposition (USP) is at the heart of all your marketing and sales efforts. It distinguishes you from the competition and can be used as a slogan. A USP is a written statement that explains why you get new customers/clients, why your current customers/clients stay with you, and why they keep coming back for more.

ACCELERATOR 8

Don't Sell What They Already Have

A LL SUCCESSFUL MARKETING—AND I do mean all—requires properly identifying your product or service as a brand, as something really needed. As an IBM ad once stated,

> **❝Don't sell what you have;
> sell what they need.❞**

When one of our daughters was about 5 or 6, she clearly demonstrated the importance of a Unique Selling Proposition (USP) based upon need, not what they already had. This cutie used to cut flowers from our neighbors' yards, walk up to their front doors, and ask if they would like to buy flowers for 25 cents.

Simply put, a USP is a written statement that explains why you get new customers/clients, why your current customers/clients stay with you, and why they keep on coming back for more and referring new business to you.

Let's examine how to proceed with building a powerful Unique Selling Proposition, also known as Unique Positioning

Statement (UPS). Although both terms refer to the same process, your emphasis should be on selling.

Three of the following companies explain their selling proposition very clearly. In contrast, even though the remaining one has a great product, this company's message does not come through.

SheTV Media:	Recreate With Us
The Junkluggers:	We Lug It All
LEATT:	The Science of Thrill
Piggycars:	Car Subscriptions, Flexible Leases, Better Than Rental

Let's break down each USP from the above list. The one for SheTV Media, "Recreate with us," does not explain that they are a video/marketing firm. In contrast, The Junkluggers' USP, "We lug it all," is a very clear message on what the company does. Although the name LEATT says nothing on its own, the word "thrill" captures the attention of those who look for challenges. Lastly, Piggycars' tagline could not be clearer.

The Heart of All Marketing and Sales—Your USP

Your USP is at the heart of all your marketing and sales efforts.

> **"Everyone is in sales. It's the only way we stay in business."**
> —Harvey Mackay

Your USP effectively distinguishes you from the competition. You can use it as a slogan. You can expand it into an elevator speech to succinctly capture the essence, strengths, and uniqueness of your product or service in no more than 20 seconds.

Most importantly, as Mickey Marraffino, owner of MMMarraffino Marketing, told me in a recent interview, "Make adjustments based on your audience but feed it into your brand."

To help you build a powerful USP, answer these five questions:

1. What is it that makes your company, firm, or consultancy stand out from your competitors?

2. Why do your clients/customers continue doing business with you?

3. What is it about your company that makes it unique?

4. Why should customers/clients come to you?

5. What do you have to offer that they cannot get anywhere else?

I Should ask WHAT?!

When your public hears the name of your company, firm, or product, what adjectives come to mind? How are you and other colleagues known throughout your community? If you don't know, I strongly suggest you ask—today.

Hopefully, the adjectives you hear describing your firm/company are positive. Look for common themes in how your peers and customers/clients describe you. Then use those themes to create and communicate who you are in every aspect of your marketing, from business development, advertising, public relations, website, social media, and even your business cards and letterhead.

Integrate this brand into your "elevator message" and encourage everyone who works for your company to be familiar with it.

More important even than asking the right questions is listening to the answers, which serve to clarify your clients' expectations and offer an opportunity to expand the engagement. When developing a USP, write down everything you have received from client/prospect calls, emails, and in-person comments. Consider calling your best customers/clients (once you have them) and simply ask them questions such as:

- What do you like about our product/service?
- Will you refer new business leads to us?
- What else would you like us to offer?

When considering what your Unique Selling Proposition might be, also involve your friends and employees (once you have them). Ask them these questions:

- Why do you think customers/clients will retain or have retained us or purchased our product?
- What do you think customers/clients want additionally?

Finally, ask your vendors, suppliers, manufacturers, and other local businesses what they think:

- Why do you think companies will want to use our service or product? If you are currently using it, why?
- What do you think can be done to improve your client/customer experience? Or, if you are still in the early marketing or selling stages, ask this: What future refinements might you consider?

- What ideas have you seen in other companies or firms that work well?

Enough Already—Now Build that USP

After all your questioning is complete, and you've compiled everything over the past several days or weeks, select the most powerful idea, the one you get most excited about, the one that keeps on coming up over and over in the previous exercises.

What is that one idea that truly sets you apart from your competition?

Take this one idea and put together a one-paragraph statement describing your new USP. It will be all over the place at this point, and that is OK. Just get all of the ideas out on paper. Do not worry about whether they make sense or not.

Now it is time to edit. Focus only on the clearest, simplest promise that you can fulfill and deliver. Remove all the extra words and make it powerful. The goal is to create a very short and compelling USP that should get you, future employees, and clients/customers/prospects excited.

Lastly, the following commonly used AIDA concept should help you finalize the USP:

- A: getting Attention
- I: holding Interest
- D: sparking Desire
- A: obtaining Action.

As Bill Aulet states in his book, *Disciplined Entrepreneurship*, "The Quantified Value Proposition gives you a concrete understanding of the measurable benefits your product will bring to your target customer."[15] Although he uses a different term, he is referring to a Unique Selling Proposition. Whichever term you choose to use, if you put in the time and effort to write one that best fits your service or product, you will more effectively present the benefits and values you offer.

Accelerator 8 Checklist

1. What do people buy?
2. How do you convert their needs to your values?
3. What benefits do you provide?
4. What solutions do you offer?
5. Identify your best results.
6. How are you building trust?
7. Remember, "Sell what they need, not _____."
8. What is your USP?

Looking Ahead to Accelerator 9: View Partnerships and Alliances with Care

In the latter stages of product or service development, financing and/or visibility and marketing reach may become a necessity beyond your individual capacity. Accelerator 9 presents options to consider, such as a partnership, alliance, licensing, or joint venturing.

ACCELERATOR

View Partnerships and Alliances with Care

I NEVER EXPECTED TO meet my future business partner and mentor walking down a prospect's hallway in Houston. From a side door, I heard, "Where did you get that jacket?" That was a real stopper. Here was a man, impeccably dressed, asking where I got *my* clothes?!

He turned out to be a competitor waiting for his chance to pitch the same prospect. Despite this, we agreed to meet in the building's coffee shop after his presentation.

Frank Mims V and I have now worked together for 10 years and have become known as the "mentors/tormentors." What our combined skills and talent brought clients/customers, dubbed "cross-pollination" by a New Orleans client, was something truly unique. He was a product sales specialist, having sold for Xerox for 25 years. Meanwhile, I focused on selling to professionals.

We brought our diverse skill sets to seminars and coaching, offering multiple perspectives on how best to approach a problem, offer a benefit, or plan a meeting. We have built both an alliance and a strategic partnership that works.

As a start-up or new entrepreneur considering teaming up with another person or firm, first, analyze what skills and experience you together would bring to the table. Consider how your potential joining would "pollinate" each of these areas:

- Industries
- Internal production
- Practice groups
- Promotions
- Business/nonprofit size and scope

Also consider where you and your potential business partner can agree and where you can find improvements in the following areas:

- Missed opportunities
- Underperforming investments
- Prospect segmentation
- Targeting
- Building effective commodity leadership

Being able to provide positive answers to all the considerations above has proven to accelerate revenue growth.

Finally, if you both decide to proceed to an agreement, make sure you clarify which responsibilities you will each lead with a view toward:

1. Do more of
2. Do less of
3. Start doing
4. Stop doing

Honestly answering these questions alone may help you decide on the need to even explore a possible alliance or partnership. However, keep reading for even more considerations.

Chips and Dips

In college, I had several jobs. My favorite one was working in the kitchen to pay for my meals. There I could also eat to my heart's content. Do you notice the ongoing food theme in my life, from frozen ice cream to deli to an open kitchen?

Our chef was also president of the local NAACP chapter, and I helped him by writing their monthly newsletter. We started a simple paid advertisement section to raise funds. I suggested to him that he advertise for party trays. He had his weekends off and could use the kitchen to make them to sell.

Sure enough, once he started to advertise, orders began to fly in the door, and his appetizers and desserts began to fly out. This was my first partnership, as we split the net revenue. Informal as it might have been, it did point out opportunities that might exist in the future. Then, when I had more control over my course schedules, I found other job opportunities which helped me get through college.

When considering some type of joint venture, you'll need to weigh several more detailed matters.

- A **joint venture** usually includes agreement on how much each invests and what the overall marketing and sales strategy will be. Profit distribution, specific responsibilities, metrics for analyzing progress and growth, and a clarifying legal agreement are musts.

- **Contracting for managing** the product or service is another option. Having another organization manufacture and distribute for you can help you remain focused on refreshing and updating your product and working on new versions. Again, legal agreements should always be utilized.

- **Licensing** is often used as a way to enter a specific market. It is designed to assign another company to use your trademark, logo, or collateral materials and to actually manufacture and sell your product or service.

- **Financial investment** is often the difference between a start-up's success or failure. As discussed in Accelerator 6, do not become so focused on building your product or service that you ignore thinking ahead and looking at all the tools you will need to access and obtain funding.

- **Become a business partner with your customers or clients.** Where you have similar goals, this type of partnership can offer a variety of benefits over many years. Demonstrate to them how you keep costs and fees palatable.

  Show that you are amenable to new ideas and new ways of doing business that help both companies. Become a "valued friend" who offers rewarding solutions that are profitable for everyone involved.

66**Seek a person of values,
not success.**99

—Albert Einstein

Clarity, Focus, Execution

Chris Frantz, the founder and managing partner of Catalina Capital, developed his business on a very careful path. It was my pleasure to be an advisor and mentor when he joined our nonprofit, South Bay Entrepreneurial Center. Chris was looking for guidance on expanding his revenue stream without adding a large number of partners or senior brokers.

After about three years, he entered a partnership with a colleague from another firm. Their approach was to be an "independent, smaller player," focusing on cost and service for their clients. They decided early they did not want to manage more than five to six people. Instead, they have developed alliances with a complementary product where both firms benefit from cross-referrals.

Interestingly enough, I heard this same approach from Lloyd Johnson, president of Chief Legal Executive and BIHC, Black In-House Counsel. When he first formed Legal Executive, several in-house legal counsels became partners and board members. His focus has always been on providing exceptional service and referrals. Both organizations agreed on the importance of working hard to offer exceptional service and spent hours each month reviewing client work.

Today, both Frantz's and Johnson's organizations are highly successful. They asked questions, looked at other organizations, confirmed their approaches, and built strong organizations.

One of the best tools available for you to evaluate the potential of a partnership or alliance is General Electric's Strategic Planning Grid, which can be found in *Essentials of Marketing* by Perreault, Cannon, and McCarthy.[16] Although it was designed to measure the strengths and weaknesses of their various divisions' marketing plans, I have adapted it to help entrepreneurs analyze their need for an alliance of some sort.

The Grid works by having you and partners conduct a very detailed review of each element to finalize a cooperative marketing plan.

Business Strengths:
- Size
- Growth
- Share
- Position
- Profitability
- Margins
- Technology position
- Strengths/weaknesses
- Image
- Pollution
- People

Industry Attractiveness:
- Size
- Market growth and pricing
- Market diversity
- Competitive structure
- Industry profitability
- Technical role
- Social
- Environment
- Legal
- Human

Lastly, with any potential partner or alliance, make sure you have discussed and agreed to the following:

- An exit strategy
- Transition planning
- Continuity planning

- Diversity and inclusion incentives
- Identity capital ownership
- Marketing and sales tactics
- Critical improvement areas
- A "break-even" point
- Internal communications

Do not let these lists overwhelm you. They are included here to provide you, the reader, with a range of questions, issues, and opportunities to use in decision-making. Spending dedicated time, including using these for evaluating direct growth completely under your own control, will be a true asset.

Accelerator 9 Checklist

1. What are your three top strengths? Why?
2. Name the concerns you have with the industry you are dealing with. How will you overcome them?
3. There are nine key segments to a partnership or alliance agreement. Do you have all nine clearly documented in a written agreement?

Case Study #4
Distribution Deals

A major cost for many start-ups that develop physical products is storing and distributing their products. One shortcut to the market is establishing a relationship with a distributor who services your marketplace, otherwise known as a distribution deal. In the beginning, Made for Success was a two-person company operating a book publishing company out of a residential home. Lacking warehouse space and shipping infrastructure, the company didn't have the essential infrastructure to expand.

The company started to research solutions and identified a distribution company called Ingram Publisher Services, a division of the world's largest book distributors. Ingram, a multibillion-dollar company representing hundreds of mid-tier book publishers, created this solution to provide distribution and sales infrastructure.

Seeking representation by Ingram Publisher Services took two years of business development efforts before being accepted. Once signing the deal, however, Made for Success instantly had access to five distribution centers domestically and three distribution centers internationally to store and sell books.

The company could also print inventory in four countries across the globe, all integrated into complex operational infrastructure for storing, selling, and invoicing. Within a short period of time, Made for Success books were available globally. Otherwise, it would have cost the company millions of dollars to build out. In return for the distribution infrastructure, Ingram Publisher Services receives a percentage of the wholesale revenues from each book sold.

A distribution deal brings numerous advantages, including decreased time to market and access to infrastructure, that is beyond the scale of a company like Made for Success. Odds are if you operate a start-up, there are distributors in your industry who can help provide the ability to scale your business at a fraction of the cost of building it yourself.

Looking Ahead to Accelerator 10: Listening Must Permeate Sales

Next to your "takeaway" message, the art of listening is the most important, effective tool in a pitch meeting. The key to your listening is to get "them" talking with carefully prepared questions.

Spending time understanding the differences between the demographics of the four current generations and learning how to sell to each will greatly assist your listening and obtaining sales success.

ACCELERATOR 10

Listening Must Permeate Sales

I LOST THE SINGLE largest engagement I would have ever landed. It would have meant excellent publicity to be working for this client as well as additional future assignments.

Training Tom, our new Philadelphia office director, I was in Wilmington, Delaware, with him for the meeting. Only 30 minutes into it, we were already discussing where we would conduct the work, who would be involved, what the final budget would be, when the recommendations would be ready, and what needed to be prepared ahead of time. We were done. The sale had been made.

That's when Tom broke in and said, "You know, I know that you want to move ahead with this, but let me tell you the two elements you are not getting." I could not stop him. He just kept talking, explaining other services we offered which were not at all relevant to the project. He did not recognize that the sale had been made, a mistake that reflected his lack of previous sales training.

Now one of our "clients" began rocking in her chair. The other prospect kept looking at his watch. Finally, I interrupted him and said, "Folks, I'm sorry. I know your time is up. We'll get back to you with our contract." But it was obvious to me we lost the sale.

As we walked the five blocks from the office building to the train station, I could not and did not speak. I was absolutely fuming! While waiting for traffic, Tom said to me—can you tell how vivid this is in my mind even today—"Why haven't you said a word?"

I won't tell you the language I used, but part of it was "… and you just lost the biggest sale you would have ever won."

During a sales meeting, it is critical to track what is being said and know when you can move the discussion into what a contract would include. Do not go back over what might have been.

Good Questions Sell Better Than Good Answers

Next to your "takeaway" message, the **art of listening** is the most important, effective tool in a pitch meeting. If you combine a frequent, powerful takeaway message along with strong listening skills, you will open up a major passage to gain new business.

IBM recommends letting your customers, clients, and prospects talk 60% of the time. Letting your clients talk more than you gives you the chance to formulate questions that best yield what their needs are. You then have the opportunity to demonstrate how best to address their needs with the benefits and solutions you have to offer.

Five Key Pre-Meeting Research Questions

1. **Who are their competitors?** Look at their industry, their products, or their services. Evaluate tax laws or legislation that might impact them.

2. **What is their business?** Understand what your prospect actually produces, how they sell it, what type of marketing they use, their management structure, etc.

3. **What are their buying habits?** Who makes the final decisions, and are they "hidden" decision-makers?

4. **What keeps them up at night?** What are their pain points?

5. **What benefits and solutions are they looking for?**

"Most salespeople are really dumb. I'm looking for someone that understands my business."

Building answers to these questions is a necessary skill in order to fully relate and understand their needs and how you address them. Remember:

"Good questions sell better than good answers."

To conclude this section, Frank Mims V, my strategic business partner, puts it this way.

"The more you listen, the more they talk, the more they buy."

—Frank Mims V,
Mims Morning Meeting

Frank, too, advises that asking the right questions, understanding their environment before that first call or meeting, and continuing to stay as current as possible on the prospect's needs, organization industry, competition, and personal background lead to sales success. His magic formula is 80/20; your goal is to first get them talking 80% of the time and listen to all their needs. Your 20% then becomes offering your solutions.

Responding to Their Answers

In the questions you develop, such as the five above, show what you have learned about their company, firm, or nonprofit. Listening carefully to their answers is one of the most important skills for closing new business.

This directly relates to the importance of understanding their needs and being able to react to them when it comes to winning contracts. Whether you have just made contact, or you are close to sealing a new sale, we cannot stress active listening enough.

It must permeate sales training, be a part of your marketing plan, and be a strategy used during every concerted sales opportunity. Listening and responding to a client's or prospect's needs is imperative if you want to score a win.

When the competition is stiff, you cannot afford to have your sales-closing skills fall flat during a presentation. Think of ways in which you can make yourself and your company/firm memorable and stand out from the crowd before, during, and after your sales pitch.

With active listening skills in place, you will have a prospect who "leans in" with rapt attention instead of one who "leans back" with disinterest or boredom.

> ## 66 Do Not Lean OUT.
> ## Do Lean IN. 99

By no means am I suggesting you employ all bells and whistles with no substance. However, a little flair won't hurt when the prospect must decide between you and another organization with similar experience.

Becoming memorable need not hinge only on a charismatic personality. While that is a factor, you should be utilizing other tools during your meetings to show you have a firm understanding of what the potential client's concerns are and what keeps them up at night.

The Five-Minute Rule

One of my clients was an in-house labor counsel for a Fortune 100 company. She had been with a law firm for 10 years prior. Having made numerous pitches herself before going in-house, she knew the type of research and approaches that would resonate.

But now, wearing a different hat, she found herself frustrated with how many outside vendors approached her, knowing nothing about their company's products and its competitors. If, within the first five minutes of a meeting, a salesperson did not demonstrate knowledge of their needs, challenges, and opportunities, she enforced the five-minute rule—out they went.

I once asked her to tell me more about her rule. She was proud to say the message was well learned by the vendors who met with her, and they "got right to it." She found a similar rule was a useful tool among her own team as well. Their meetings got right to the point, did not waste anyone's time, and resulted in clear and concise decisions.

Eat Your Fingers Off

Key messages, including your "takeaway," must be encoded in a manner that the recipient can then decode and interpret the desired message clearly. A humorous example where this did not occur was when Kentucky Fried Chicken was entering the huge market of China. A translator converted (encoded) their well-known motto "Finger Lickin' Good" into Mandarin.

Unfortunately, early customers (decoders) interpreted it as "Eat your fingers off," and you can just imagine the uproar that mix-up caused.

It goes almost without saying that groups interpret messages differently. Using the correct message channel requires careful preparation. This certainly applies to your brand, as well as to the messages you are offering in your sales calls and meetings.

Encoding a clear message is even more complicated today because selling your product or service may be of interest to any of the four major generations currently vital and active in our world.

- Baby Boomers, born between 1946 and 1964, are a group with significant incomes and looking for solutions in selecting products and services.
- Gen X'ers, born between 1965 and 1977, are a much smaller group than the Boomers. With their kids no longer a main focus, their tastes for products and services are in flux. Selling to them requires more detailed research on specific needs and concerns.
- Gen Y, the Millennials, were born between 1978 and 1994. They are beginning to collect savings and work well with technology. Concerned with costs, they spend more time analyzing purchasing options, waiting for sales or specials, and want to see others successfully using the product or service before committing.
- Gen Z refers to those born since 1995. They think and act online. They are called "digital natives" and want to hear from you by text, cell, Zoom, etc. Pay very close attention. As this group matures, they will have a greater impact on the economy and be in control of significant purchasing decisions.

Most likely, your product or service will require completely different sales approaches depending on which generation you're marketing to. You may limit your targeting ultimately to only one or two of these groups. Spend time researching the surveys and demographic details of each group and take special note of their differences. These will impact how you specifically tailor the need and use for your product to them.

Nos

Hearing a "no," "not interested," or "not at this time" is an important key to future success. These rejections present opportunities to rethink what you are presenting and how to meet these types of challenges in the future.

During my first career in city and county management, I met my second mentor, Bill Wagstaff. He was the personnel director of our 5,400-employee county with an annual operating budget of $400,000,000 and could be described as a "no guy." Whether initiating a new program, negotiating with 13 different unions, or identifying communities where the county might build a new health center, Bill made sure all aspects were considered before a final decision was made.

He taught me how to be a chief executive, pay attention to details, and stay in frequent communication with senior staff and the elected officials. He also showed me when it would be timely to promote, i.e., sell a new program. He knew how to employ the rule of "knowing thy client" well.

When Bill retired, many were quite surprised with the person I appointed to fill his very large shoes. When some asked me about my choice, I said it was because our new director could also say **"no!"** By that time, I had seen the benefits from Bill's willingness to do so. Through seeking counsel from advisors prior to making decisions and having support staff feel all viewpoints were welcome, the decisions he made were generally well thought out and effective.

Listening to trusted advisors prior to decision-making is an absolutely necessary practice. As Sir Winston Churchill once said, "Standing and listening is not listening. Sitting down and listening is the sign of a leader."

If, after all your efforts and preparation to make a sale, you get a "no," do not stop there. Remember that **maximizing rejection**, a concept previously discussed in Accelerator 4, is one of our rules that recognizes how much the potential customer/client has invested in you, just as you have in them.

Stay in touch. Send them updates, ask them to be on conference panels with you, and remind them how much you can contribute to their business or nonprofit. Keep yourself in the closing zone, creating opportunities for a future "yes."

> **❝Beware of Zombies, those who don't see the value of communication.❞**
>
> —Tom Ziglar

Focused Listening

Scott Hogle, a business executive, successful author, and a new mentor to me, wrote a remarkable book, *Persuade: The 7 Empowering Laws of the SalesMaker.* His concept of **focused listening** comes from years of successful sales experience as president of iHeart Radio Media in Hawaii.

He identifies the following five requirements for effective, focused listening that a salesperson should employ in every setting:

1. Patience
2. Concentration
3. Attention
4. Reciprocation
5. Conversation[17]

When you are ready to expand your sales skills and make your product/service a revenue success, make sure you read his book.

❝ Value is exchanged on both sides of a conversation when focused listening occurs. ❞

—Scott Hogle

Notice that his list includes a **conversation**, which is a mutual exchange of ideas, challenges, obstacles, and solutions in a sales setting. This word likewise appears in sales pitch recommendations from several successful entrepreneurs. In fact, one of my newer business colleagues, Sheila Miller-Nelson, the managing partner of Midian LLC, recently told me that she recommends using a "conversation format" as the best tool to engender trust, gain important information, and reach a successful conclusion.

She uses this concept as a key ingredient in her training seminars. It provides a format for that all-important tactic, future relationship building.

Accelerator 10 Checklist

1. Get your client/prospect talking _____% of the time.
2. Have you prepared questions ahead of time?
3. How well do you know their business?
4. What are their pain points?
5. Why do they do business with you?
6. Have you learned their buying patterns?
7. Good questions sell better than good _____.
8. Convert their needs to your _____.

Looking Ahead to Accelerator 11:
Don't Confuse Sales with Marketing

Marketing is used to identify customers/clients, to get them paying attention to your product or service, and to keep their interest in buying it. It involves understanding their needs, wants, opportunities, and challenges.

For start-ups and new entrepreneurs, you need to begin thinking about marketing your product or service as you approach the "proof of concept" stage of development. You are the focus of this book. Make sure you do not make the mistake of concentrating so much of your attention on what you are building that you overlook who will be interested in it and how to ultimately reach them.

ACCELERATOR 11

Don't Confuse "Sales" with "Marketing"

M Y VERY FIRST lesson in marketing came at age 16, on the very first day of my very first job—I was hired and fired. It was at a Dairy Queen where I couldn't get the soft-serve ice cream to swirl, which was and is their hallmark. Selling squashed cones did not deliver on their marketing promise. So, after eating my mistakes and having the manager explain how I was contributing to lost revenue, off I went. The good news was that down the street was a deli that hired me as a grill chef. As a bonus, they offered plenty to eat.

Marketing comes in so many forms that people often confuse it with selling; however, it is clearly not. Let's clarify the distinction between some commonly used terms:

- Marketing is getting found.
- Business development is selling.
- Business generation is "closing" the sale and building relationships.

Thomas Miniere of Miniere & Company, in a YEC Council post, provides a definition that proves the point about mixing marketing and selling: "There have been several instances when my agency has generated leads for a client only to have that client struggle to turn those leads into revenue. This is often indicative of a sales problem, not an advertising problem."

The same post follows: "Marketing is a broad term and includes not only the advertisements used to get leads, but also the sales strategy that turns those leads into action by a customer..."[18]

I could not disagree more since sales strategy, as stated above, is separate from a marketing strategy. Even *Wikipedia*'s definition of marketing also includes sales, calling it an "integrated process."[19] Again, I could not disagree more for the same reason: sales is not marketing.

In my experience, "marketing" evaluates needs of a customer demographic, translates this information to the producers of the product or service, uses a wide range of methods and media to reach the appropriate customer channels, and works to build a relationship with this target. Marketing is used to identify the potential customer, keep the customer paying attention to the product or service, keep their interest in buying the product or service, and understand the needs and wants of the customer.

Keep in mind, mature markets and overcapacities in earlier decades caused the evolution of "marketing." Prior to World War II, production of goods and services was able to meet demand. There was little need to market or "create demand." As the post-war economy grew and manufacturing became capable of producing a larger volume of products, companies then shifted their focus from production to the customer in order to stay profitable. Plus, since many markets are individually idiosyncratic, they require special insights and marketing approaches to successfully penetrate.

The Four "Ps" of Marketing

For entrepreneurs, understand that marketing is comprised of the **four "Ps"**: Product, Place, Price, and Promotion. Notice that none of the four say anything about sales. Rather, marketers consider **product** areas such as service, benefits, instructions, packaging, and branding (see Accelerator 1 for branding details). For **place,** entrepreneurs need to consider areas such as market exposure, channels of delivery, and obtaining market exposure. **Price** receives input not only from marketing but also from production, shipping, and inventory. Finally, **promotion** may include advertising, publicity, supporting sales specials (not selling), and especially highly focused use of social media.

Moreover, in a recent presentation, David Ochi identified the following 10 types of marketing:

- Digital Marketing
- Inbound Marketing
- Content Marketing
- Social Media Marketing
- Search Engine Marketing
- Advertising
- Influencer Marketing
- Affiliate Marketing
- Email Marketing
- Word-of-Mouth Marketing

Other marketing tactics include:

- Outbound Marketing
- Organic Marketing
- Outreach Marketing
- Guerilla Marketing
- Referral Marketing

- Nostalgia Marketing
- Public Relations
- Voice Marketing
- Seasonal Marketing
- Stealth Marketing

For early start-up marketing considerations, as you define your initial market and the demographics you will be focusing on, selecting one of these 10 will get you started. As your business grows, adding more of these will directly contribute to growing revenue.

The Top Three Marketing Myths

As a new entrepreneur with a start-up, you need to begin thinking about marketing your product or service as you approach the "proof of concept" stage of development. As a consulting mentor for numerous start-ups, I urge you to not make the mistake of concentrating so much of your attention on what you are building that you overlook who will be interested in it and how to ultimately reach them. Carefully take what you read here and make sure you do not fall for the following marketing myths.

Myth #1: *Sales and marketing are interchangeable terms.* Again, marketing is about being found, not chosen. How you get your new product or service found is through publicity—media outreach, networking, collateral materials, conducting and attending workshops—that targets the eyes, ears, and interests of your potential client or customers.

Myth #2: *One size fits all.* News flash, one size never fits all. In reality, a diverse set of skills and approaches are needed to accomplish a business goal. Marketing needs to be tailored, business development requires sales training, and closing skills will land the new business.

Myth #3: ***Don't wait to begin marketing.*** Start-ups need to begin testing the marketplace during early product/service development and continue to consider what benefits and solutions their creation might truly bring to future customers/clients.

Elevate Your Chances of Success

In a recent conversation with me, Nanneke Dinklo, the director of marketing for a $100,000,000 brand-packaging company, made the following observation. In her experience working for several major companies and serving as a volunteer mentor for new entrepreneurs, she has observed that you can never start soon enough thinking about your potential marketplace, pricing to meet the customer/client target, and how you will bring it forward.

Remember to ask yourself these questions: What problem are you solving? Do you have your customer segment clearly defined? Will you have an advantage over competition, and how will you be reaching out to your customers/clients?

This is marketing.

66Create a sense of demand rather than waiting to hear demand.99

—Barbara Corcoran, *Shark Tank*

"When I was in college,
marketing meant going to the grocery store."

You Can Never Start Marketing Soon Enough

Let's take a closer look at Nanneke Dinklo's observations above. As you are refining your new product or service and moving closer to implementation or production, consider the following:

1. If you are solving a problem, how do people's needs fit in? Will you need to produce options, different levels of skill or features, to address the four different generations you might ultimately sell to? Will you need to also consider operational characteristics such as demographics?

2. Have you carefully addressed the customer segment your product or service is being designed for? How will you be presenting your "creation" to them? Are there legal considerations to ensure the formal approvals you will need in order to reach your customers/clients?

3. In the energy and excitement you have while developing your idea into reality, consider who your competitors will be, how you will differentiate your product from theirs, and even how they market and sell.

4. When you begin looking for financing or setting up beta tests for your product or service, successful marketing (and sales) requires a UPS, a unique positioning statement, often also called a USP, a unique selling proposition. This direct group of 10 words or less is the "takeaway" message you want to present to your marketplace (discussed in detail in Accelerator 8).

   It is your brand.

66 Your UPS is at the heart of all your marketing and sales efforts. 99

With a good UPS, a longer version can turn into your 20-second elevator speech. This UPS is at the core of your future marketing efforts. If it isn't, you will be giving up one of the most powerful sales weapons within any company's arsenal: uniqueness.

66 Marketing should not be left just to the marketing department. 99
—David Packard,
Founder of Hewlett Packard

Building Your Business

During the development stages of your great idea, you can begin studying the market with a few simple, non-time-consuming approaches. These will place you in a position to make that future business of yours successful. We introduce our clients to the following most basic trio of marketing knowledge resources:

- Go
- Know
- Read

You are probably active in, or should be active in, professional and industry groups. They can easily provide you with marketing guidance by going to where they go, getting to know whom they know, and reading what they read. If your future prospects for selling your product or service to are at these meetings, begin finding out about their backgrounds and start building relationships with them.

Make sure you are reading the relevant journals, papers, and social media sites to stay as current as possible. Your future marketing plans will be building a referral base that becomes critical in introducing your product or service to buyers who are considered "early adopters." Many of these referrals should come from your reading and follow-up actions.

Use Hidden Sales Tools for Marketing

Successful salespeople use "hidden" sales tools that marketers should also practice. For you in the early entrepreneurial stages of building your future business, begin practicing these tactics as you Go, Know, Read:

- **Permission Marketing:** This means obtaining a prospect's okay to contact them without appearing to be marketing or selling. For example, when you are talking with a new contact at a meeting, and she/he expresses interest in a particular topic, mention that you have seen a helpful article on the topic and suggest sending it to them. When they say "yes," and they will, tell them you'll call in a week to make sure it is interesting and helpful. You now have their "permission" to follow up.

- **Invisible Marketing:** This looks to draw a prospect or customer in to assist you in a way that also compliments them. As you get closer to presenting your new product or service to the marketplace, send your new collateral materials or social media draft posts to prospects you have met or to current clients/customers you may have for your other business.

    By explaining how important their opinions are to your future success, you have complimented them. Whether they respond or not, you have reached out to them in a way that they will remember.

- **Cross Marketing:** This is where alliances with other companies can really pay off for you. Accelerator 17 contains a more detailed discussion on this topic. But developing an alliance with a non-competitor to market and sell together will widen the opportunity to expose your product/service in an expanded group of prospects and industries.

- **Conversion Marketing:** In the book by the same name, Bryan Heathman, the publisher of Made for Success, presents a new way to look at online marketing. His book includes 16 psychological tools that describe how to influence the buying behavior of website visitors. Bryan brings his marketing experience from Microsoft, Xerox, and big-brand marketer Eastman Kodak.[20]

For cutting-edge marketing campaign ideas, even while your product or service is still in production, read *Conversion Marketing*. It will reinforce your early recognition of future techniques and tactics that will help you succeed.

Accelerator 11 Checklist

How does your marketing plan address each of these?

1. Economic buyer
2. Overlooked assets
3. Hidden assets
4. Opportunity mindset
5. Value creation
6. Customer experience
7. Unique selling proposition
8. Competitor analysis
9. Marketing strategy

Case Study #5
Backend Functionality

Joining us at this point of product development was Kyle Winkle, Made for Success's research and development manager. He brought the necessary computer skills, social media applications, and experience in constructing the complex backend functionality and user flow necessary to make the *Growthbook* education programs work.

Combining with Bryan's and David's experience, Kyle outlined the steps needed for each of the following:

- User/subscription management
- DRM management
- Payment gateway
- Title usage reporting (royalty reports)
- Title completion and issuing a "badge" when each skill is learned

At each weekly Zoom meeting, we discussed two of these functions in great detail. The most critical of these was ensuring the user experience was positive and simple. For the student, it starts with the login and finishes with earning a badge and moving on to the next series of lessons. For colleges and universities interested in providing this for students, each lesson contains a PDF with a series of questions to aid student retention.

Each course would require 10 essential steps:

- Login
- Welcome
- Home
- Course Outline
- Course Page/Progress

- Course Player
- Course Complete
- Course Quiz
- Awarding of Badge
- Accomplishments

At this stage of development, "active" debates continued over several weeks on matters such as subscription fees and payment options. The development team made necessary decisions as their backend functionality progressed. Still, several unsettled issues continued:
- User Settings
- Payment/Billing
- Subscription Additions/Edits
- Completed Courses
- Badge Downloads

It was during several of these and previous discussions that we decided on the product name, *Growthbook*. We wanted students to know from the beginning that completing the coursework would enable them to "grow" their sales skills, pipeline, and revenue streams.

Setting page features for future subscribers was the next step. After we identified the need for the course player and the PDF quizzes, we followed up with steps to implement the home screen and course page.

From here, our individual assignments doubled with product development becoming the primary focus.

Looking Ahead to Accelerator 12:
Build a Proposal Roadmap

Understanding the marketing basics that will help guide completion of your product or service leads to the next discussion—getting ready to sell. You now have a marketing strategy to accompany and help formulate the key elements of what you begin proposing to prospects. Note that this is a strategy, not a marketing plan. According to a past *Economist* commentary, 95% of marketing plans remain on the shelf.

> **"Use advanced tactics and process strategy, not theory."**

ACCELERATOR 12

Build a Proposal Roadmap

A S A VOLUNTEER mentor for start-ups during the past 11 years, I often heard new entrepreneurs comment, "Once my product is developed, I'll find someone to market it." They were so wrapped up in the development phase of their work that they had given no thought to who would want to buy it and how to reach them.

Our South Bay Entrepreneurial Center pre-cohort interview teams used one overriding criterion to decide whether or not to accept a candidate into our program: Are they coachable?

Had they even thought through how their product or service would address the need they were targeting? How would they describe it as a solution? Clarifying this link between a client's need and the solution you describe is often the key to winning new business.

These mentees became my inspiration for writing this book. They needed significant education and help to move into the goal of becoming profitable. In a recent discussion, this goal was succinctly offered to me by Bryan Heathman:

"Churning Product Development
To
Churning Revenue Development."

This accelerator and the next two provide the tactics and strategies needed to plan, propose, refine, rebuild, and close new business.

I Am Now Your Accelerator Coach!

Your first lesson is to study this list of 14 Best Closing Skills Practices.

1. **Opening Arguments First**
   Don't concentrate on the minutiae and hope it drives you to a stunning conclusion. Start with your UPS to explain to potential clients. Your basic message should be this: "Here's what I can do for you, here's how we are going to get there, and let's discuss the details."

> **66Start where you are.**
> **Use what you have.**
> **Do what you can.99**
> —Arthur Ashe, Professional Tennis Great

2. **Give Something Away**
   Once you are face-to-face with a prospect, you should be talking strategy and providing advice on how the transaction might be completed. This strategy must give the buyer a concrete sense of what it will be like working with you.

3. **Underscore Accountability**

   The way you sell products and services should directly reflect the way you work internally. If appropriate, propose regular meetings and include budget reviews as items on every agenda. Make the buyer feel just how assiduous you are in keeping them aware of what is happening and how much it is costing.

4. **Dump Your Resume**

   Ideally, you should never talk about your company once you are face-to-face unless it is specifically relevant to the prospect and you are directly addressing their needs. One of the complaints I often hear from clients and seminar attendees boils down to this:

   "I know about the damned number of professionals that they have. I want to hear them talk strategy and production. I want to see how they think."

5. **Let Them Talk**

   In Accelerator 10, "Listening Must Permeate Sales," you learned that when they talk, they are engaged. Remember the IBM 60/40 rule to get your client talking 60% of the time. Good questions sell better than good answers.

6. **Deliver Value**

   By the time the meeting is over, buyers should understand more about their own situation. As a result, when they retain you or buy your product, they will feel all the more confident about the decision.

7. **Understand Needs**

   Another common complaint I hear from buyers is that "prospectors" don't really understand what they need. What are the pressures going on inside their company, agency, firm, or nonprofit? Have their competitors introduced a "market busting" new product? Knowing answers to questions such as these will help inform your approach.

66Build a competitive advantage.99
—Frank Mims V,
Mims Morning Meeting

8. **Identify Hidden Decision-Makers**
As previously discussed in Accelerator 2, in order for you to overcome hidden decision-making, your strategy must include a systematic approach to finding out what the decision-makers won't reveal on their own.
- Who is the real buyer?
- Who is the real user?
- Is the person at your meeting actually the real decision maker?

9. **Evaluate Relationships and Retention**
By now, you, the reader, must know the importance of relationship building. How have your prospects made past vendor selections? What problems did they encounter? Has there been any press or media coverage of the relationships they have or had?

66Engaging prospects a must.99
—Sir Richard Branson

10. **Learn Their Personal Concerns**
Closing strategies demand not just objective data on an organization's retention patterns but also maximum personal and subjective sensitivity to the man or

woman across the table from you. What are his or her individual hopes and fears, and how can your firm/company play to those, for the client's benefit as well as your own?

11. Focus on Selection

Don't ever assume that just because a company has retained a competitor of yours for many years that they would not be willing to consider a change. In fact, offering to undertake a quick, simple, and low-cost project is often the way into more work. Do compete in situations where you might otherwise assume the competition has an insurmountable advantage.

When a buyer presents a specific problem to you, ask them how they would like to see this issue handled. Doing so achieves extra yardage because you are inviting a more substantive discussion—and showing that you intend to really get down to business, to talk strategy and not merely promote yourself. Right away, the buyer has the expectation that the meeting will produce value for her/him, irrespective of which firm/company is eventually hired.

> **66The very expectation of value creates a dynamic that's optimally conducive to closing. 99**

12. Ask for Their Business

When was the last time you asked your customers directly for their business? On the surface, that question may seem redundant. After all, once an organization has signed on with you, it might feel a bit silly to ask. But consider this: Asking for more work on a semi-regular basis is a solid client retention tactic that could lead to bottom-line dividends.

Make sure you are conveying the confidence that you can assume these new tasks. Ask for the work. Demonstrate to the client that your firm/company has the capabilities beyond the scope of your current project, and then lay out how you can help them clearly and concisely.

13. Think Business Generation and Value

If the new work involves a fledging area your company would like to promote, use warm relationships with your client to persuade them to take a chance on your company rather than a competitor more established in this area. Sweeten the deal and negotiate a lower cost for a set time period—perhaps three to six months—so the customer can gain confidence in your ability to successfully handle the project.

"I've failed once before — Why try again?"

14. Maximize Rejection

That's right, maximize rejection. If, after all the effort and preparation of your proposal, you get a "no," do not stop there. Maximizing rejection is a concept that recognizes the potential customer has a lot invested in you by the nature of the time and study they put in during the selection process. After you hear an initial "no," you still want to do these things:

- Stay in touch
- Send them updates
- Ask them to be on panels with you
- Remind them how much you can contribute to their business

> 66 **Teach advanced tactics and process strategy, not theory.** 99

Emulate These Positives

In meetings and pitches, taking a confident, positive approach is an important tool to stimulate an open discussion. Accelerator 14, "Supercharge Your Actions," provides details on the positives.

"We always miss the major new trends."

Here are a few you can use immediately when calling on prospects.

- Set the call or meeting agenda up-front.
- Start with a quick overview of their need and your proposal.
- Underscore how you will be communicating with them.
- Let them talk.

Keep your clients and prospects ahead of economic and industry trends. Remember that offering something extra helps to differentiate you and your organization from the competition.

Look for ways to help your prospects and clients, once you have them. Offer to make introductions, suggest alliances, or find new relationships that could add to their bottom line.

Anticipate generic problems, not just client-specific ones. Keep them ahead of the curve.

Remember, your prospects, clients, and customers have careers, too. Reward them by providing opportunities to lead, speak, and co-author articles. Their company reaps the benefits, and you become even more key to their success.

❝Growth and comfort do not co-exist.❞

—Ginny Rometty,
CEO, IBM Corporation

Accelerator 12 Checklist

1. What am I missing in pre-sales knowledge?
2. Who are the most critical prospects?
3. Who are their competitors?

4. What are their buying patterns?
5. What is their most significant need?
6. How often have they retained other firms/agencies?
7. Do you know how to maximize rejection?

Looking Ahead to Accelerator 13:
Build Launch Readiness

Once your proposals are ready, you'll need to consider multiple factors when beginning face-to-face selling. To assist in making your preparations simple but thorough, I will present key implementation tools and continue to emphasize the importance building relationships. The new world of selling to four different generations requires understanding their differing needs, communication preferences, and attitudes. Lastly, I explain the 21 keys to driving successful performance.

ACCELERATOR 13

Build Launch Readiness

WITH ONLY TWO weeks under my belt, working for a new company in a professional service area in which I had no previous skill or experience, the company's COO asked me to fill in for him for a major speech. It was to be in front of an audience of over 300 senior executives.

After a cram session on the topics, I asked the COO to give me the key points that needed to be covered and cited at least twice. I practiced with a small group of our staff, hopped on a plane, and gave the talk early the next morning.

There was a smattering of applause, which I thought was the audience just being polite. That is, until someone came up to me and said he wanted to learn more. It became the first new engagement I landed and encouraged me to learn more about growing my speech skills.

I wound up selling, that is speaking, an average of 50 times a year. So did others in the company as it grew into 12 offices throughout the U.S. Watching competitors and other professionals speak, sell, and communicate taught me the importance of focusing on two to three key takeaway points and practicing in front of my colleagues.

What also helped me was going to Susanne Egli, a professional speaking coach. She had previously advised me I needed to smile more and add humor. Her message now was simple: "Just get out there!"

Practice Lunch

In the seminars we lead, "practice lunch" is not a throwaway line. It means even if you are only going to a prospecting lunch, practice the agenda, your questions, and possible responses.

You have everything ready, so go! One major asset you have is your takeaway. No matter what else people remember or don't remember from the meeting or conversation, it must be this core message.

Do not walk into a meeting cold. Practice your agenda, key points, and takeaway message with one of your colleagues. This message is the **differentiator** for you and your firm from your competitors. You can word your takeaway in slightly different ways, but make sure to mention it often during the course of your discussions.

Five Keys to Successful Meetings:

1. **Anticipate** the answers to your questions. Prepare answers for their questions.

2. **Understand** their business. Identify key elements of their business, their competitors, their products, and their services.

3. **Build trust** by letting them know you care about their business. Have your primary points ready, including that "takeaway" message.

4. **Keep in front of them.** Don't be a pest, but if you read a relevant article, send it to them with a short note.

5. **Always set the next contact.** There is a marketing concept called "Permission Marketing." When you ask for a time and date for the next contact, and they agree, you've obtained their "permission" to sell to them.

   And whatever the key is that you want them to remember, keep in mind this quote from Jeff Bezos, the founder of Amazon:

❝Your brand is what stays in the room after you've left the room.❞

Now that you've practiced, get out there.

Why Hasn't She Called Me?

A client approached me one day while in an intense, all-day workshop with a question: "I negotiated a highly successful contract for my client six months ago; why hasn't she called me? We got everything she needed. It will earn them a fortune of money. Why hasn't she called me?"

I was honest with my response: "In six months, after such a successful engagement, you should have initiated contact with her at least twice, including sending a small gift as a reminder of the 'win.' Second, you had started to build a future pipeline. Shame on you for not capitalizing on your success."

Stay in touch regardless of how successful your work has been for them. "Why hasn't she called me?" should never be in your vocabulary because you have been following up.

You have "the ask," you have gone through all the steps, and you are out there. Your follow-up skills are in place. When you are ready for new business, where do you go? You should know the answer—go to your pipeline.

But in case you don't, a Harvard Business blog reports that 50% of your new business every single year should come from clients/customers, referrals, and prospects that are already in action with you.[21] I did not attend Harvard but have found their sales material exceptionally useful. One of the discussions they cover is the importance of **returning to past clients.**

> **"50% of your new business every single year should come from customers, referrals, and prospects."**
> —Harvard Business Publication

We should note a few additional points. Tony Robbins, a highly recognized motivational/marketing speaker, along with one of his top colleagues, Chet Holmes, published the book *Business Breakthroughs*. A good read, this book emphasizes that 80% of the time, it takes at least five contacts before you will win new business—at least five contacts.

> **"80% of the time, it takes at least five contacts before you will win new business."**
> —Tony Robbins & Chet Holmes,
> *Business Breakthroughs*

Think about where you are with current leads and opportunities. Recognize how important clients and referrals are because these people know you. Perhaps revisit the sources you used to find past clients? If you have not stayed in touch, do so now. They are a means of adding to your potential revenue base. There are such things as a phone, Google, Zoom, fax, or email, remember? You can use one of these relevant scenarios—adopt one and use it.

GO, KNOW, READ
OR
FIND 'EM, MEET 'EM, GET 'EM, KEEP 'EM

Generational Selling

What else do you need to do? We've talked about what people really buy; we've talked about pre-sales knowledge that becomes important. But here is another element that you must consider, and it is most unusual.

As I've mentioned before, there are four different generations that you are now offering your business and products to—four different generations. Let's describe a bit of their tendencies and then talk a bit about how to sell to each.

Since there are now more selling channels, you need to really refine how you present information, presentations, and proposals.

Baby Boomers are ages 55-73. They work hard, are primarily first generations, and are also the first generation that has a significant number of **women in the workforce.** This group wants to hear solutions.

Gen-Xers are ages 38-54. They believe strongly in a **work/ life balance.** It is the first generation that looked closely at how to balance these two components of their lives. They are really enjoying life now.

Gen-Y, Millennials, are ages 25-39. As a group, they are impatient, dress casually, and deal with people in a very casual way. They are extremely environmentally and globally concerned; acknowledging this fact will add strength to your sales approach.

Gen-Z, the "I" Generation, are those ages 24 and below. This group is very pragmatic, great at multitasking, and digitally programmed. But keep in mind, if you prospect with this group, be prepared to meet a 24-year-old millionaire/CEO.

When selling to any of these groups, you must keep in mind what type of presentation you need to make, how you should structure the discussion, etc. It's critical to understand each generation's different values and who they, in turn, are selling to.

Are they selling only to their same generations, or have they learned how to sell to the others, just like you need to do? Who are their competitors, and how do they compete? Based on their characteristics, do they compete differently? What are their buying patterns, and are or how are these integrated into their organizations?

Lastly, know how active each of your prospect groups is on social media. It's a great topic of discussion, an early series of questions to ask, and helps you take their "needs" into your "values" and translate them generationally.

As mentioned earlier, we urge our own customers, clients, and prospects to practice, practice, practice. Before you make a presentation, before you prepare an email, before you even draft a proposal, practice with someone. How does the wording come across, considering the generation of the prospect?

Practice, practice, practice.

Boomers prefer **solutions-oriented selling**. Gen-X'ers prefer **value-based selling**. Gen-Y'ers, the Millennials, prefer **digital selling**. Gen-Z'ers, the newest generation, want to hear from you on Twitter, Instagram, etc., in other words, **social-media selling**. Keep in mind you will not be successful unless you listen, learn, and practice.

The 21 Keys to Driving Performance

Building an action plan is the key to your future success. You will refer back to it, modify it when challenges and opportunities occur, update it as you learn more, and use it to keep your entire marketing and sales efforts on track.

1. Don't let yourself be overwhelmed.
2. Evaluate all ways to build relationships and then select one and work on it.
3. Always have questions ready to ask clients, prospects, and new contacts.
4. Learn more about their businesses, companies, and nonprofits.
5. Ask what your support team can do to help their business growth efforts.
6. Refine and update your UPS and elevator messages.
7. Determine what others can do to assist you.
8. Identify all the various tactics available to you to pitch your business. Then select those most capable of helping you win the new contract. Known as the Force Multiplier Effect, it emphasizes that you often have more tactics to employ at the same time, rather than approaching a prospect with only one. Doing so will many times increase the chances of winning the new engagement.
9. Make multiple uses of a single effort. If writing an article, convert it to a presentation, send it to the press, send it to clients, put it on your website, or make it an e-alert.
10. Measure results, timing, expenses, and ROI.
11. Practice your pitches, proposals, and lunch.
12. Schedule regular update calls with your current clients.
13. Pick one sales tactic and then start to work on it.

14. Use pre-meeting calls and contacts to agree on an agenda.
15. Obtain commitments and agreement on next steps.
16. Learn what your competitors and your prospects' competitors are offering.
17. What can you "give away"?
18. Make sure you determine any price sensitivity.
19. If you choose not to respond to an RFP, call and let them know why.
20. Learn their selection criteria.
21. Understand their decision-making process.

The most successful entrepreneurs I know use this or a similar checklist on a monthly basis. They set aside an hour per month to turn off the phone, hide from their computer, close the door, and not accept any "got a minutes" from anyone.

Since you are "out there" too, make it a mandatory practice to anticipate, understand, build trust, and stay in front of the implementation keys to a successful acceleration of revenue.

Accelerator 13 Checklist

1. What am I missing in my pre-sales knowledge?
2. What generations am I selling to?
3. Whom are my prospects and clients selling to?
4. Who are their competitors?
5. What are their buying patterns?
6. How active are they on social media?
7. Am I practicing with my colleagues?
8. What is my "takeaway" message?
9. What is my differentiator?
10. Have I anticipated questions and answers?
11. How can I use "permission marketing"?

12. How often are you repeating the "takeaway"?
13. "Your brand is what stays in the room after you
    _____."

Case Study #6
Product Development and Standard Operating Procedures (SOPs)

"Who said it would be easy???"

Continuing with more and more necessary tasks to develop the product, a Standard Operating Procedure (SOP) became critical. In Month 8, we began looking ahead to Month 11 with the possibilities of introducing our product to major industry national and international conferences. Pressure increased, and we had to identify and track task assignments.

David Ochi and I developed a preliminary SOP for implementing the *Growthbook* series. Made for Success added tasks to that. Given the preliminary timing of Month 9 (with a bit of stretch room), we considered building our first effort focused on post-Spring Break. We also contemplated offering a "semester pack" to a select pilot group and asking for feedback.

Discussions became more heated and intense as each team member presented his opinions. Cost and implementation timing forced us to finalize many approaches.

Here were our 17 final implementation tasks:
- Content management
- Website design/final branding
- Technology tools start-up
- Affiliate program setup
- Social media management
- Royalty management
- Pricing determination
- Training interns and others
- Prepping reporting and monitoring systems

- Marketing and sales materials
- Alliances/affiliates
- Initial course distribution/initial contacts
- Conference and trade show bookings/speeches and booth (costs, staffing, travel)
- Beta test sites
- "Boot camp"
- Financial budget, revenue tracking
- Subscription renewals/offerings

Once we finally reached agreement, each of us took our assignments from this list, developed our SOPs, and continued to target Month 10 to produce our first minimal viable product (MVP).

Very difficult final decisions followed.

Looking Ahead to Accelerator 14: Supercharge Your Actions

This accelerator includes the top tactics for successful prospecting, dealing with "closing" new engagements, and what prospects are really looking for.

ACCELERATOR 14

Supercharge Your Actions

ONE OF MY earliest sales lessons was during the oral defense of my doctoral dissertation. After driving into New York City from New Jersey two to three nights every week for four and a half years, completing all those classes, taking four intense days of subject exams, and writing the dissertation, it was the final-final.

The newest Ph.D. of the six examining professors asked me what I thought was an absolutely stupid question. As I was about to bark back at him, my mentor and advisor, Dr. Perry Norton, reached across the table and put his hand on top of mine. He leaned over and whispered, "Just shut up."

The biggest lessons I learned from that experience were to better prepare, anticipate questions, and know who was going to be at the table and their reputations. I should have researched the subject specialties of each professor more, especially the one who asked that question. Since I did not have him for a class, I should have talked to students who studied with him. These lessons have translated again and again to my own selling experiences.

Recently I participated in a brainstorming session with a group of professional salespeople. The focus was on how to improve selling. Even though we all represented a wide variety of industries, we reached an agreement on which marketing and sales tactics were the most effective.

The top six tactics for successful prospect engagements that emerged from this brainstorming session are the following:

1. Be prepared
2. Talk with, not at
3. Test your approaches
4. Have one "takeaway"
5. Do not repeat yourself
6. Utilize "active listening"

Engaging with prospects enables you to show your investment in working with them and is as crucial as your message when it comes to generating new business. Let's continue learning how to engage and increase sales by adding substance to your presentations and pitches.

The Fine Art of Closing

Sales is a multifaceted process in which, painfully enough, the most formidable moment occurs at the end. All the laborious efforts to reach the goal line may be in vain if you, the seller, have not mastered the art of actually asking for the business or if you do not sufficiently understand the dynamics that will maximize the likelihood of a positive response.

> **"The art is named 'closing,' and it is a fine art indeed."**

Are you ready to "make rain" and search for customers and clients? To build a good, measurable sales roadmap, use the suggestions in this book which provide turn-by-turn guidance and show the most direct route to finding and "closing" prospects face-to-face.

Having spent 35-plus years working for companies and firms, I have a deep understanding of how the owners and principals make their buying decisions. I've had the opportunity to "look from the inside out," so to speak. As a result, I present to you, as a provider of a service or product, the roadmap elements on how to generate new business rapidly.

In selling, there is a critical point at which strategy and tactics dovetail. As a result of your relationships and the trust you engender, you need to build a key message—that what you are selling is a "must-buy"!

> ❝In selling, there is a critical point
> at which strategy and tactics
> dovetail...❞

This message is fundamental for closing any significant sales transaction. Once you are in a "closing zone," establishing your product or service as a "must-buy" is the key deliverable for people whom you may be selling to—many of whom are risk-averse and sales resistant.

The savviest marketers will tell you (and what we tell our clients) is that the "closing zone" refers to the time you, the seller, are meeting with prospects one-on-one after all your pitches are complete. This is where you will be using the closing skills you've developed to win new business—the final destination of your sales roadmap.

“New business is the final destination of your sales roadmap.”

Prospects you are selling to will often have two opposing fears in their minds. One is the fear of the sales process itself, their fear of being manipulated, being sold a bill of goods, or of debasing their professional integrity by being part of the "promotional culture."

The other fear is of lagging behind or not being able to match their competitors or serve their clients or customers with the best in products or services. In some industries, it might be not working with the newest equipment to increase production speed and efficiency, or applying state-of-the-art information systems to improve client communications, or having a market-savvy website. The list goes on and on.

Your job in selling is to ensure that the second fear overpowers the first, that what you are selling is not only a nice-to-have but a need-to-have, and that, by partnering with you (not just buying from you), they are making an investment in their own success.

Competitive Combat Coaching

Sometimes you may require a more introspective, robust, and productive way of looking at growing your sales successes. This book focuses on the importance of you having your strategies and tactics practiced and ready. For an additional perspective, I would suggest Jay Abraham's book *Getting Everything You Can Out of All You've Got*. Here, Abraham suggests a sometimes-necessary program called "Competitive Combat Coaching."

This effort urges you to look to the number of tools that you are not using effectively. The more you look at your own organization—with or without the help of a business development consultant—the more you are going to find each of these:

- Underperforming assets
- Overlooked opportunities
- Hidden assets
- Undervalued relationships
- Underutilized collaborative opportunities[22]

When the competition intensifies, and client budgets fight to stabilize, doesn't it make sense to look within your organization, build on what is already there to have it make more of an impact, and then win the combat/competition you face?

The cost to you is low, and the effort will make you more effective.

Why Should I Hire You?

Never forget that you are essentially asking someone else to hire you for your product or service. Ask yourself, "why should they?" Refining the execution of your sales strategy and upgrading your assets are excellent starts. But, in addition to doing all of that, you must also consider other questions running through your buyers' and prospects' minds.

1. Do you know what is happening in our marketplace?
2. Can you possibly understand the pressure I'm under?
3. How can I measure your results?
4. Can you describe the risks I'm taking if I hire you and your firm/company?

5. What do you know about our competitors and their products or services?
6. How will you typically provide us updates and information?
7. How can you support me in my dealings with the executives and board of directors?
8. How do you bill?
9. Who are the people you will assign in staffing this engagement?
10. What are your expectations for earning new business?
11. Tell me three reasons why you are better than Firm/Company X?
12. Beyond your diversity committee, what do you really do?
13. Do you understand how we communicate internally?

Kick-Ass Revenue Signals

In Accelerator 5, I discussed 11 mistakes that offend businesspeople, in other words, tactics that do *not* work in sales. However, the same group of business executives I participated with to compile that list have also highlighted what *does* work in selling. Take the following 12 tactics to heart and make them a regular part of your sales approach:

1. Make a major effort to communicate at the beginning of an engagement.
2. Quickly deal with problems and complaints.
3. Offer annual seminars with great material.
4. Refer business to your customers/clients, introduce them to each other, or cross-sell with them.
5. Send contact information ahead of meetings showing the agenda and who else will be there.
6. Mine your children's activities for potential prospects and future referrals.

7. Set periodic review meetings regarding budgets, billing, and timelines of the process.
8. Make periodic non-business contact with customers/clients.
9. Make your client/customer look good.
10. Deal respectfully with all their personnel.
11. Provide references for your clients.
12. Ask your clients for referrals and introductions.

Here's one last clue for you in building your sales roadmap. Bryan Heathman discusses a new way to look at online marketing in his book *Conversion Marketing*. This book is loaded with fresh ideas for cutting-edge marketing campaigns aligned with a selling campaign. He concludes with 16 Psychological Tools of Influence that describe how to influence the buying behavior of website viewers.[23] Read it.

Only Five Minutes Per Week

Most firms that approach my company looking for business development and sales training want fast results. Many of them are surprised when we say that a dedicated five minutes per week is all it takes to put a plan in motion. For instance, consider these examples:

- It takes five minutes a week to make a phone call to touch base with a client or prospect.
- Five minutes a week is long enough to send an email to a prospect, client, or customer.
- In five minutes, you can arrange an in-person meeting or a Zoom.
- You can commit to writing an article and jotting down a list of possible topics in five minutes.

The actions themselves will take longer. But by dedicating just five minutes to each business generating tactic, you will be implementing your sales roadmap marked by true efficiency and will be on the path to accelerating revenue.

Accelerator 14 Checklist

"Why Should I Hire You?" questions:

1. Do you know what is happening in our marketplace?
2. Can you possibly understand the pressure I'm under?
3. How can I measure your results?
4. Can you describe the risks I'm taking if I hire you and your firm/company?
5. What do you know about our competitors and their products or services?
6. How will you typically provide us updates and information?
7. How can you support me in my dealings with the executives and board of directors?
8. How do you bill?
9. Who are the people you will assign in staffing this engagement?
10. What are your expectations for earning new business?
11. Tell me three reasons why you are better than Firm/Company X?
12. Beyond your diversity committee, what do you really do?
13. Do you understand how we communicate internally?

Looking Ahead to Accelerator 15: Build Your Acceleration Funnel

The need to provide a simple, visual tool to assist in building your base of prospects, customers/clients, set sales priorities, and close new business is next. It is now time to go out and "ask for the business."

ACCELERATOR 15

Build Your Accelerator Funnel

THE ACCELERATOR FUNNEL is a visual tool designed to keep you on track and display where you are each day. Here's the simplest way to look at the Accelerator Funnel and put it to work. It is not a complex Client Relationship Manager software system (CRM); rather, it's an aid to help you build a base of prospects, customers/clients, and referrals, set sales priorities, and close new business. It is a visual crunch without the clutter.

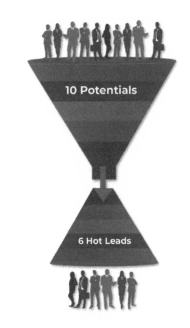

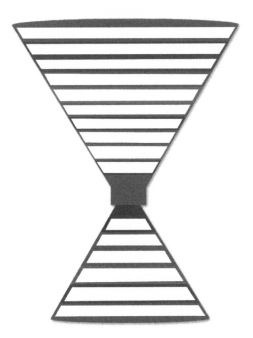

THE REVENUE ACCELERATOR

Picture it—take what we've learned so far and combine it into three elements that will go into your Accelerator Funnel:

- Customers
- Referrals
- Prospects

You should be working with every single one of them, and the product of the funnel is asking for their business.

As a review from Accelerator 11, make sure you understand the difference between marketing, business development, and business generation. These terms are not interchangeable.

Marketing is about getting found, i.e., website, social media, publications, speaking, and similar activities.

Business development is selling when you are out in front of prospects and agencies, at service firms and organizations, and trying to convince them to buy.

Business generation is closing the sale. The objective is **"the ask,"** asking for business by accelerating your business development and business generation and speeding the decisions along. These three major steps, as I emphasize in my previous book *Own the Zone—Dominate the Competition*, get you to the bottom line, the "ask."

The "Ask"

This is where you want to be with every person you are meeting, talking with, or emailing. Follow a prescribed series of steps from the very first handshake. Note that you do not have to utilize every single step. If you have worked with someone before, these are options. You can remind them of the past work/product/successes or just go through the steps as reinforcement. If it is a new product or service offering, keep in mind where these steps might help.

Take all your clients/customers, prospects (met with or identified), and referral sources, build three separate lists, and prioritize each list with "most recently contacted" or "most likely to need," etc.

Next, select a total of 10 from each of the 3 lists where you have the best chance of winning business now and contact them by setting meetings, Zooms, or calls. Once they have been set, move them out of the top of the funnel into the lower "action" funnel for follow-up and closing. When a contact is moved out of the top funnel, bring the next one in.

> **❝Always have 10 leads in the top of your Accelerator Funnel and move them into the 'action' funnel.❞**

Keep in mind, the Accelerator Funnel is not a "plan." A "plan" just sits on a shelf. According to a past issue of *The Economist*, 95% of business and marketing plans just sit on shelves.

Instead, using the Accelerator Funnel will give you weekly, organized actions which will have you selling, not sitting on the "shelf." The more you use the Accelerator Funnel, the more opportunities you will have to "ask" for business.

Managing Me

You've got the "go"! Put the Accelerator Funnel to work for you now, today, and with any support team members you have added. In his book *Persuade,* Scott Hogle says it best:

66 The biggest challenge I have ever had to manage has always been myself. I have found that the better I get at managing [myself], the more control I have in creating success around me. **99** [24]

—Scott Hogle,
Author of *Persuade*

The Accelerator Funnel is all about providing a way to manage yourself, stay organized, and have a workable system right in front of you at all times. My own sits on my desk always reminding me to act.

Two quotes from my firm's clients illustrate the value of using the Accelerator Funnel. First, Tim Pierce, the owner of a special product manufacturer, said this: "[The Accelerator Funnel] helped guide us in identifying the most lucrative sales channel and selling our newest product. Initial results included the sales of 100,000 units to Disney theme parks."

In addition, Chris Frantz, managing partner of the Catalina Capital Group, gave this positive review: "[The Accelerator Funnel] helped our professional services firm generate significant revenue increases. The training assisted in clarifying client priorities, leading to spending more time with the right prospects. An all-around winner."

Make copies of the Accelerator Funnel pages at the beginning of this chapter, begin entering your priorities, and move on out to start "asking."

Accelerator 15 Checklist

1. List your top 10 customers/clients.
2. List your top 10 referral sources.
3. List your top 10 prospects.
4. Now, list your top 10 leads from all of the above.

Case Study #7
Interim Decisions

Our team was making decisions on an as-needed basis, primarily on the backend software structure. We agreed upon a preliminary pricing format and began writing the intern job description and recruiting. We also considered a "micro-start-up," eight-week course and established a website and email identities. As a group, we identified initial testing sites for the first version. Then we narrowed down possible partnership/ affiliations with other universities and colleges to several options. We contemplated the value of soliciting a corporate sponsorship and gave thought and attention to sign-up bonuses for early subscribers. We even finalized the design of our business cards.

One of our toughest decisions was due to budgetary constraints, as we concluded that we could not yet afford to become a sponsor of the first major professional conference to be held in Month 11. An early launch just wasn't feasible.

At this same time, the end of Month 9, we identified and made other decisions, such as finalizing the initial four badge requirements:

- Negotiation Skills
- Closing Skills
- Prospecting Skills
- Relationship Selling

We developed a PDF of questions after each lesson in response to colleges and universities interested in providing this as an aid for student retention. We also began recruiting for a script narrator.

We narrowed down and finalized the "takeaways," our Unique Selling Proposition, to these broad advantages:

- Content partnership
- Higher education content
- Badging capabilities from a major university
- Exclusive access
- Start-up/entrepreneurial focus

However, we were yet to make concluding decisions.

Lastly, text was presented aimed at new subscribers to the *Growthbook* program, and all four of us agreed and wholeheartedly endorsed the following content:

Congratulations! You are now part of a learning community that can empower small business owners by providing access to education and resources. This program is about helping businesses like yours thrive. It'll teach you digitally savvy strategies other businesses are using to get ahead.

1. **Learning Modules**: Brief, information-packed lessons that give you strategies you can use right away. These interactive courses can help you learn new skills and increase your business knowledge.

2. **Coaching**: Guidance from business experts who can help you apply what you know and what you're learning to build and execute your plan

of action. Experienced mentors and subject matter experts will provide practical guidance in both group sessions and personalized coaching specific to your situation.

3. **Community**: Online opportunity to share information with other business owners, build your network, support each other, and engage in potential projects together. Connect with a community of learners who share your interests. Learn, share, and grow your network with other like-minded entrepreneurs throughout your learning journey.

4. **Incentives/Offers**: Benefit from an exclusive marketplace of tools, solutions, products, and services that can help move your business forward. Gain eligibility to apply for an exclusive pool of grants that you can use to boost your business growth.
Log in and start your journey today!

Looking Ahead to Accelerator 16: Follow Up, Follow Through

Following through with actions useful to retain your customers/clients, the types of decisions needed to grow your business and actually assisting your clients with their operational problems are the primary lessons that are in the next accelerator.

ACCELERATOR 16

Follow Up, Follow Through

Y OU ARE AT go. You are out there. They have said "yes"; they want to proceed. What do you do now? The contract is in your hand. They've signed it. You've got it "locked."

Understand that this might be the best way to lead into new additional business, as long as you keep working on building those relationships. Once you have spent the **customer acquisition cost**, keep those customers.

To do that, look to tactics most entrepreneurs are unaware of.

Implement the following techniques during engagements and beyond to retain your customers.

Eight Actions to Keep Customers

1. Commit to helping them thrive.
2. Offer to co-market with them to their prospect.
3. Apply "invisible marketing" techniques as we've discussed earlier in this book.
4. Keep adding benefits.

5. Clarify what is working well and what needs improvement.
6. Develop a post-acceptance checklist.
7. Continue building the relationship (ABR).
8. Don't forget to send thank-yous.

Make sure your connection with them continues to flow smoothly. Remember that story of the client who waited six months for her client to call after a successful engagement? That was really poor judgment on her part. Just because the client was pleased with the work is absolutely no excuse for not staying in touch.

Growth Actions Program

As your customer/client base grows, it becomes equally important to look internally at your organization and where you can identify future growth opportunities or eliminate bottlenecks to revenue enhancement.

23 Growth Actions

1. Decide what's effective, what's not utilized, and how you can enhance your impact.
2. Discern any industry focus that offers special opportunities now.
3. Build a broader marketplace by offering your clients/customers something additional.
4. Track new customers/clients. How many of your services or products are used by each, and do they use them each year?
5. Seek to build new business from primary industry groups or identify and pursue new groups.

6. Make sure you know which current and future clients/customers actively track diversity of women and minorities in their engagements.

7. Take note of the frequency of new client transactions for additional services vs. longer-term clients.

8. Know your clients' turnover ratio for CEOs, purchasing agents, etc.

9. Decide if the creation of a "top client" relationship program would be helpful.

10. Ask how valuable "brainstorming" meetings with clients/customers would be, at no cost to them, on a periodic basis.

11. Determine if top-of-company executive visits would be helpful.

12. Know who might replace your clients if they leave, are terminated, etc. Start courting them, or perhaps consider making this the responsibility of other team members.

13. Track lead sources. Use this as a tool to measure the success of future outreach efforts.

14. Consider an internal, informal success/rejection discussion for leads won, lost, or put on hold.

15. Test drafts of new materials, speeches, presentations, and articles with current clients. This can be a good relationship builder and an "invisible marketing" opportunity.

16. Actively search for opportunities to serve on advisory boards, professional associations, or community organizations where clients will also serve.

17. Target professional conferences one to two years out and get on program committees and chair sessions.

18. Meet with editorial staff of major and/or local papers and business journals. Suggest topics, surveys, etc.

19. Identify and build references from your core clients.

20. When updating succession planning, include business development effort and success, understanding of client economics, and client management skills.
21. Consider having one or two primary charity and pro bono approaches for the year.
22. Offer to speak at conferences and community organizations; make commitments work harder by getting your name out there and being highly visible.
23. Make sure you know which active and prospective clients are intentionally involved in encouraging diversity and inclusion of women and minorities and support them.

Put Yourself in the Story

Whether you prefer to read the *Wall Street Journal, Houston Chronicle*, or a local paper in the morning, or listen to or watch other news sources, or follow your favorite social media site, you'll learn plenty of economic news. The Dow is up, and then it is down, for example.

But you aren't the only one reading and listening. Your customers, clients, employees, and future employees scan and listen to the same business information that you do.

Why not give them something to talk about? Utilize this tried-and-true selling technique: Put yourself into the story.

66Put yourself into the story.99

Social media today offers you the chance to present yourself and your company/product/service as a credible source regarding issues affecting your area of expertise. This is an appropriate time to use active business development techniques in media relations. You could comment on employment, industry trends, or new product availability, to name but a few.

You provide the perspective and intimate expertise that reporters need to move their stories. But if the *Wall Street Journal* seems way out of your league, opt to be the big fish in a small pond and contact reporters at your local news sources and in your social media groups.

Become a "go-to" person, and your name and product/service will appear in future articles, establishing trust. When people see your name and read your quotes, your credibility will soar. That's a value advertising just can't buy.

Transform Your Clients' Liabilities into Assets

Surprise, surprise, your clients and customers have careers, too. They need friends to help advance those careers. They want to be thought of as leaders, too. Here are some surprising ways you can assist them.

Help them impress their bosses. If you are pitching something new, offer something beyond assurances of work quality and cost control. Make it substantially more strategic so that a senior executive can use it as an internal selling tool for themselves.

Look for ways to help your customers, clients, and even solid prospects make friends. They are often bombarded with requests for guidance from business unit executives as well as departmental managers who want to "get things done" without exposing themselves or their company. If you are proposing a new system, for example, look for opportunities to communicate how you would efficiently support them with guidance.

Anticipate generic problems, not just company-specific ones. Can you communicate how you might help your contact become an internal problem solver for such challenges?

Help generate business for them. Make introductions, suggest alliances, and find new relationships that could add to their corporate bottom line. You have other customers, and you know people throughout their industry or in industries the client has targeted for expansion.

Invite in-house decision makers to a luncheon program and sit them next to people with whom they can develop mutually beneficial relationships. This is sending a strong but subtle message about the overall professional advantages of working with you. Remember, they have careers, too.

Don't Squander New Opportunities

The tasks you face to win those first contracts and keep battling for more may seem like one large obstacle. Keep in mind the selection factors and contact tactics that drive new business. Purchasing agents and business leaders have gotten much tougher and demanding, rightly so, especially in light of how inexplicably resistant so many companies are to improving their own deliverables.

More than one businessperson has told me that they generally assume that long-term client/customer relationships do not require additionally heightened service levels. You already know how costly this can be. At least you should be asking what else you can do to assist the client to ensure continuing engagements.

Your competitors create new opportunities for you every day simply by falling down on the job. Particularly for smaller companies that base their survival strategies on client/customer service, an enticing new business pool is now accepting applicants. It would be a shame to squander such opportunities by falling back on old excuses.

Don't squander such opportunities. Now is the time to market and sell by overcoming client resistance and offering an innovative carrot or two to pique the buyers' interests. In any event, the real takeaway is that every impediment to business development can be transformed into a business development tool.

> **❝Every impediment to business development can be transformed into a business development tool.❞**

For the tech-savvy, there are great opportunities to reach primary markets. On social media sites, ask your own questions, offer responses, contact the questioners, and link them to your LinkedIn, Facebook, Twitter, and Instagram.

Be resourceful enough to make the critical difference between you and your competitors.

Accelerator 16 Checklist

1. What will help you build more business?
2. Remember ABR.
3. Have you committed to help your clients thrive?
4. Remember to offer to co-market.
5. Ask to meet others in their firm/company.
6. What benefits can you add?
7. What is working, and what can be improved?
8. Have you developed a "post-closing" checklist for your team?

Looking Ahead to Accelerator 17:
Don't Accept Bad Excuses for Not Selling

If you are the one-only salesperson, or have begun building a team, excuses for not getting out there and selling will start. They will be intelligence-defying, self-sabotaging, agonizing, or even honest. Convert them to revenue generation or move them aside.

ACCELERATOR 17

Don't Accept Bad Excuses for Not Selling

HOW MANY PEOPLE have you met or heard of who could "sell anything"? It's not magic. Yes, some people are born to sell, but 99% of successful salespeople have spent years honing their craft and learning from experts.

But do you still hear excuses from team members not wanting to sell? Whether you are managing a sales team, are a one-only salesperson, or are indeed part of a sales team, somewhere along the line, you must have accountability. Excuses for not selling will not be tolerated.

How does this apply to whoever is leading the sales charge? They or you should be committed to accomplishing every single day. You must be "on" all the time. Keep a very simple lead tracker to make the effort easier and assist in accountability—and to see results. Here are some of the most common categories of EXCUSES:

Nine Self-Sabotaging and Agonizing Excuses for Not Selling

1. "I may not have the right skills." Then how were you appointed to this position in the first place? Did you discover this quickly, or were you left on your own for too long?

2. "My partner does all the selling. I just do the work."

Yet the person who does not sell most likely is working with members of the clients'/customers' organizations, knows them, and can be coached to implement simple marketing tools.

Recall that this was the problem with the $10,000,000 account leader who never worked himself at staying in touch with many contacts he had. He had also never encouraged or directed his staff to build relationships with these contacts.

❝It is the responsibility of client-relationship leaders to ensure that everyone in their group builds relationships with their peers at customer/client organizations and in professional associations.❞

Identify who would replace your contacts if they left their positions or if the company was acquired. Invite them to be on a panel with you or ask about co-authoring an article that would then appear in their industry journal.

3. "Nothing I'm doing is working." But when you ask what specifically they are doing, like writing an article of interest, they vaguely reply, "Well, it's just not working."

   You need to recognize and deal with these excuses before the selling begins. Address them and straighten them out immediately. Or do not have those making the excuses as part of your sales team. You do not need excuses from people who do not want to sell.

   "I don't want to pester people." People that say this need to understand that they are not pestering. If a sales team member can offer a solution to a real need, he will reach that prospect. But if the potential client does not return phone calls or emails or does not communicate after a meeting, at least the seller gave it a "try."

4. "I'm very busy." Well, aren't we all very busy? As a sales manager, this explains why you must keep current with what the team members are engaged

in. Do a quick review of their time-spending. If, in fact, they do have actions that need to be delayed or postponed, make sure those still remain in their funnel.

5. "I can't market, but I'll hire someone who can." Let's hope the people making this statement are actually doing high-quality work. Consider colleagues in production, accounting, human resources, and reception as your support team. They can ask others, such as suppliers, for introductions. Ask for referrals. Invite them to meetings of your industry association. They do not have to "sell."

"I can't market, but I'll hire someone who can."

The quality of your work can be a valuable calling card, even if you have not used it before. Evaluate your prospects, prioritize them, and begin a contacting approach. Have questions ready to ask them; learn more about their business or agency; ask how marketing tactics can help with your business development efforts. Build a contact list and feed it into your Accelerator Funnel.

66Finally, practice your pitches, proposals, and even lunch.99

6. "I don't need to sell. My revenue keeps on coming in." Well, isn't that sweet? But again, recall the story from Accelerator 2 about the client who lost a $10,000,000 account and then realized he never followed up with any other contacts he'd had. It never occurred to him that he needed to build a client base outside this one engagement. So, when the client fired him, he panicked.

   Ensure that your sales team members are contacting their "revenue sources." They should be regularly asking their clients questions like these:
   - What more can I do?
   - Can I come out and meet with you?
   - Will you introduce me to others in your company, your business, your industry?

7. "I get good results; what else is needed?" Are you now at the stage where you have core customers? If you are, have you reached out to them for a recommendation? Clients and customers who have achieved excellent results from your product or service should become your best referral sources.

   "Another thing to consider here would be inviting your customers and prospects to any charity or nonprofit events you are involved in. You know these people, and they know you—so ask. Doing so shows them your concern and participation in organizations designed to help others. Including them at fundraising dinners is a benefit to socializing with them."

Ask those core clients to introduce you to others in their company, agency, or even to their senior executives. Test drafts of new materials, speeches, presentations, and articles with current clients and prospects. These can be good relationship builders and "invisible marketing" opportunities.

"Honestly, I don't know how to begin."

8. "Honestly, I don't know how to begin." Often, we are asked questions like these: "What resources can I turn to that will cultivate more referrals? Are there simple instructions to help me find new clients/customers?" The following suggestions may seem elementary yet are often overlooked by even experienced revenue builders.

If you see a client or her company mentioned in a journal article, clip it and send it to them with a handwritten note. How about keeping in touch with college classmates? If you are on local boards of directors, offer your professional or technical expertise or get active on a program committee.

Give decisive preference to those foundations and boards with current or prospective clients whom you may be selling to in the future. As always, remember to be continually building relationships.

> **❝The secret of getting ahead is getting started.❞**
>
> —Mark Twain

9. "My customer's business keeps changing, and I don't keep up." Sellers miss many opportunities to communicate effectively and track their clients' companies and industries. Is it any wonder that clients terminate such a high percentage of long-term relationships?

If you are not using your identity capital, such as your brand, USP, and values to the fullest, your position will slip. As discussed in Accelerator 4, one of my firm's clients recently decided it was taking on too many small projects that were encroaching on the time available for more profitable clients. They utilized Peter Drucker's "Creative Abandonment." By organizing and implementing a plan to phase out or transfer clients, they began spending time with higher-yielding clients. More importantly, from an ethics position, they ensured the former clients continued to receive top skill assistance.

Transform your business culture, erase artificial boundaries between sales and service, and understand the bottom-line benefits of speaking directly and honestly to customer needs. Smart companies have adopted top customer teams and ensure annual visits. They track who might replace their current in-house engagement leaders and make sure members of their team are actively building relationships.

Building your own internal succession plans for each client/customer will also provide more attention to each. Another way to stay current is to attend a client's industry conference and read their journals.

> **❝Remember, go where they go, know whom they know, read what they read.❞**

Head-nodders

When Mary Barra, the president and CEO of General Motors, was first appointed, someone asked her what her major challenge was. Her succinct answer may seem surprising:
"Head-nodders."

She was referring to employees who, when asked to accomplish something, nod their heads "yes." However, when they then walk out of the room, they simply go about doing whatever they had been doing before.

Her solution to the head-nodder problem was really simple. She said,

> **❝People need to know the 'why' in order for them to do the 'what.'❞**

Finally, here are other excuses I have heard as it pertains to head-nodders:

- I'm afraid of the process.
- I won't cross-sell.
- I'm not compensated for selling.

- We have no training program.
- I know no one who knows anyone.

Make sure you explain the "why," or you may have real difficulty seeing results. As you think through excuses your team is presenting to you, keep Mary Barra's observation about the head-nodders in mind.

You do not need to hear excuses. Spend more time with sales training so that the team can transfer what they are doing into revenue generation. If they can't generate revenue, you may need to move them aside. The bottom line is that you must have total reliance on the team.

Accelerator 17 Checklist

1. You are accountable for _____.
2. Implement a simple lead tracker.
3. Turn excuses into action or change their responsibilities.
4. Consider Mary Barra's observation about the "head-nodders." Are you explaining the "why" to your team?
5. If you don't see the numbers you expect, look deeper.

Case Study #8
Facing the Unknown

"We have no training wheels."

Moving into Month 10, none of us had ever built a product like *Growthbook* before. We did start with the great news that our website went live. Additionally, in a major step, we successfully opened a Topflight app.

But we had not anticipated the need to overcome a growing number of tasks. For the new apps we began using, finer details and complications required us to set up links to our other apps, such as for our user database, payment integration and processing, and email setup. Once we accomplished this task, we needed to refine our website accordingly. In addition, we now had to identify university business schools to test our pilot apps and schedule meetings with them.

Our team began spending more time closing in on blending the systems and apps. Month 11 remained our target for initial testing.

Looking Ahead to Accelerator 18: Don't Drive Clients Crazy

Accelerator 18 provides important steps you should take to avoid what does not work in meetings; for example, don't be boring and formulaic in your presentations. Learn from the clues to avoid driving clients crazy.

ACCELERATOR 18

Don't Drive Clients Crazy

IN SURVEYS MY firms conduct in the U.S. and Canada involving executives, business owners, marketing directors, counsel, and others, the single number one problem they have with pitch meetings is **how boring they are**.

Do you remember the movie *Groundhog Day*? Bill Murray's character lives the same day over and over and over. That's probably what it feels like to hear the same boring sales pitches on a regular basis.

You want to do better. After reading the next story, you may want to think of the number "13" when you're crafting your next sales pitch.

Every day a man walked the same route to work, passing by a mental institution with a very high wooden fence. Each day at that spot, he would hear from the other side, "13, 13, 13, 13, 13," from the men and women. They were chanting the same boring thing every day.

One day he was finally tired of trying to figure out why they were repeating "13" over and over and decided to peek in.

Locating a knothole, he looked inside and got poked in the eye with a stick. Then he heard "14, 14, 14, 14, 14."

> **❝Again, the number one complaint that we hear consistently is how boring pitches are. Keeping that in mind, strive to make sure what you say and write sounds fresh and new.❞**

Don't Just Get 'Em; Keep 'Em

Scott Hogle reminds us of the importance of client service in his book *Persuade*. He writes, "Many companies are great at teaching sales strategies and closing skills to win business, but sometimes neglect the skill of keeping and reselling existing clients."[25]

Once you have won customers or clients, now devote a measurable amount of time to keeping them. During the sales process itself, let them know how you will be working with them and what positives you will bring.

In previous chapters, we discussed tactics and skills needed to bring in business. Many of these strategies also help in preventing sales breakdowns or maintaining a buyer. Several include how to avoid driving clients crazy. Let's do a quick review.

Nine Ways to Avoid Driving Clients Crazy

1. Make sure the level of Client Experience (CX) you build offers a deep value. Customize your approach, remembering that "one size does not fit all." During the sales process, ask the prospect what they expect on an ongoing basis, and then describe how you will customize it for them.

2. Recall Jay Abraham's three primary reasons clients leave from Accelerator 3:
   - Lack of contact
   - Dissatisfaction
   - A change in their situation

   Communicating on a regular basis, both during the sales process and once retained, should avoid the first two issues. By building a relationship over time, you should have built up enough trust to learn about changes before they impact your project.

"Our suppliers are spoiled and dull.
I want to shake things up."

3. Don't use a "formulaic" sales presentation that appears memorized. You don't want anything that feels like PowerPoint slides simply moving forward. Prospects can tell almost immediately that your pitch has not been customized for them and will become bored or cut the meeting short.

   A "consultative" sales format emphasizes what you have learned about the company, industry, products, or services and blends in how you can offer benefits to their needs. Plus, you will be leaving significant time to ask them questions and listen closely to answers.

   Their needs will be front and center, and you will be actively engaging the prospect.

4. One of the most customer-annoyed complaints we hear about sales pitches is that "They were trying to sell us what we already have." Once your business is growing, make sure you and your sales team don't make this or similar blunders. Avoid questionable jokes, stay off cell phones, and don't send too many people to the meeting.

5. When beginning to use your new Unique Selling Proposition (USP), listen and watch carefully. Are prospects confused, or is it too long? When you repeat it during the meeting, do they appear to recognize it? Have they asked questions about it or asked you to clarify an element? Remember, it is your "takeaway" message, the one key you want them to recall.

   Having encountered situations myself where prospects became disinterested in the discussion, I learned to take a chance and ask them what wasn't clear or what was confusing in my discussion. While not always winning a new buyer, I certainly learned how to be more precise in describing our services.

6. Ignoring the 60% rule—getting your client or prospect talking at least 60% of the time—will often create a sense of boredom in the prospect's mind. By constructing highly relevant questions about their concerns, issues, and pain, they will have a chance to express their needs directly to you.

   This also offers you the opportunity to repeat the "takeaway" message, overcome any loss of prospects' interest in the pitch, and stay top of mind. They will also understand more about their own situation and more confident about the buying decision.

7. Don't use the same sales approach for a Baby Boomer that you use for a Gen Z'er. They think differently, want the information in different channels, and will likely shut you off before a meeting even gets scheduled. Gen Z'ers are digitally programmed to send and receive information. Details that a Baby Boomer would find important would likely be irrelevant to the Gen Z'er.

8. Don't delay responses. If you have been asked for something or committed yourself to delivering something, get it done fast. If it is something like a proposal that will take time, let them know and keep them posted. They may be making commitments to others in their organization relying on your timely response.

9. Prospects and customers are also concerned about a possible overcapacity to deliver. Can you deliver on time? Will you be relying on others to complete the work in a timely fashion?

Think through these types of experiences and problems that drive clients crazy. Train your sales teams accordingly—and have them practice.

Accelerator 18 Checklist

1. Remember the Groundhog Day syndrome. Is your pitch boring?
2. Are your responses to your client prompt and accurate?
3. Have you overloaded your customer with information?
4. Are you avoiding what does not work in meetings?

Looking Ahead to Accelerator 19: Maintain Virtual Meeting Etiquette

Mind your manners, make sure you know the time allocated for the meeting, and bring solutions and benefits to your prospects.

ACCELERATOR 10

Define Your Virtual Meeting Approaches

I N PREVIOUS CHAPTERS, we've touched on social media and virtual services as they relate to building awareness of your product, providing details on its applications to prospects, and where you can be reached for further information.

But do remember that although virtual services should not replace the importance of in-person contact, they can be a huge asset if used correctly. Presented here is a series of observations by expert marketers on virtual meetings and refining the uses of social media.

Don't Throw Jell-O Against the Wall

Scott Herring, the founder of Twisted Puppy Media and a colleague of mine at mentoring new entrepreneurs, offers a unique view about using social media and virtual meetings:

"The difference between marketing today and marketing when I started (way back when) is that we have better knowledge now of what works. It's no longer like throwing Jell-O against the wall. Good marketers have frameworks, create hypotheses, measure results, and learn to grow their businesses. You can't hide like old-school marketers could. All the old techniques can still be employed, but they need to be verified."

Scott refers to how much more experience and analysis we have now of what works and doesn't work when using social media. "Way back when," as the internet marketing resources were expanding, marketing professionals were trying every new tool without a level of sophistication on measuring results.

Alice Heiman, an absolutely brilliant marketing and sales guru and teacher, presents another view to consider. It was tweeted by @Forbes, where she is often quoted.

❝Many businesses are focusing on automation and remote interaction. But some in-person human connection could seal the deal.❞

Alice recognizes that even in this Zoom era, and with Gen Z'ers who prefer to deal primarily online, the goal of building lasting relationships continues to need in-person contact.

Nanneke Dinklo, the marketing director of a $100,000,000 personalized packaging company, sees the value of an e-commerce site as a virtual asset.

> **❝An e-commerce site never sleeps, always takes orders, and never gets cranky.❞**
> —Nanneke Dinklo

It does not need salary, fringe benefits, or vacations and therefore keeps the customer acquisition cost at a minimum."

Most importantly, it is always there to capture inbound communication from prospects.

In my previous book, *Own the Zone*, I name social media as one of the best tools available to identify and evaluate businesses without those companies even knowing these assessments are taking place. Yet face-to-face meetings that end with handshakes remain critical for at least two of our current generations, Baby Boomers and Gen X'ers.

Accelerator 5 noted a recent British Airways advertisement that read, "Emails don't end in handshakes." Their goal, of course, was to get you to fly across the pond on their planes. But the basic message of this advertisement is valid for any type of business, as Heiman points out.

Recall the discussion earlier in this book about encoding and decoding messages. Millennials and Gen Z'ers are fully adept at sending and receiving messages electronically. Most do not need person-to-person meetings to close a deal.

Make sure your marketing and sales programs are appropriately adjusted to the targets and their need or understanding of electronic presentations.

Getting Through the "Noise"

Marketers and advertisers are familiar with a concept identified as "noise." This consists of every type of interruption that can intercept a communication channel, especially those online. Pop-up ads, news flashes, new message forwarding, even eating in front of a computer can distract viewers/potential customers from the messages.

When addressing this issue at seminars and coaching sessions, I often hear complaints that include confusing websites, too many messages, and misinterpretations of a tagline. Recall the problem Kentucky Fried Chicken had when their famous slogan "Finger Lickin' Good" got mistranslated as "Eat your fingers off" by the locals they were trying to market to.

One simple tool, taken from the book *Essentials of Marketing*, that you can use to overcome noise and improve your communication channel is to clarify your promotion objectives, which fall into one of the three following categories:

- Informing
- Persuading
- Reminding[26]

In other words, make sure your messages are focused on one of these objectives at a time. If you are introducing a new product or service, concentrate on "informing" the marketplace about it and how it works. Make the descriptions simple and clear, leaving the "reader" wanting more information.

The second phase of your promotion is to modify your campaign to "persuade" readers to want to learn more. Make sure your Call to Action (CTA) stimulates and builds contacts from those readers who have now become prospects.

Third, once sales have begun, modify your campaign again to remind prospects and those who typically buy early that others have seen the value and benefits of your product/service.

By following this approach, you will filter out much of the "noise" for those you draw into your new product's uses and value.

- Go Where They Go
- Know Whom They Know
- Read What They Read

Go Where They Go

For a new entrepreneur, going virtual is a quick, relatively lower-cost way to obtain early exposure for your product or service. At least two of the current buying generations, Baby Boomers and Gen X'ers, value one-on-one time that in-person meetings provide.

Certainly, electronic communications have all made it much easier to stay in touch with your customers and clients. But if you believe emails, cell phones, Zoom, and social media are the only paths to retaining clients and facilitating closing skills, you need to think again. One-on-one meetings still have a high value for customers and prospects, primarily the two older generations mentioned above.

The marketplace is crowded, and competition is fierce. However, savvy firms and companies understand that an unprecedented level of opportunity is still available. By building a strong online brand, shifting to client-centric communications, making it easy for prospects to find you online, and engaging with social media wisely, you will be taking steps in the right direction.

This is why a major theme of our book is to get you thinking about marketing and selling during the development stages of your product or service. As David Ochi, director of the Innovation Incubator at California State University Dominguez Hills indicated previously, "Look at your potential market first, determine if there really is a need for your new idea, and then—and only then—begin developing it."

Accelerator 19 Checklist

1. In addition to social media and virtual meetings, how often are you setting in-person meetings?
2. Which generations consider face-to-face meetings necessary?
3. How many of the tools to overcome "noise" are you using to enhance your promotions?
4. What tactics are you using or considering in order to reach the two most digital-based generations?
5. Can you measure the success of your online branding?

Case Study #9
The App is Live

At the very end of month 10, the *Growthbook* app went live. Adding it to our phones was an absolute thrill for all of us. Although the app still needs refinement, we are close to our first beta tests.

We have begun testing our pricing and licensing parameters, identifying additional resources for marketing and sales targets, completing the first quizzes that follow each learning segment, and finalizing unique graphics.

Most critically, our long-range **strategic plan** is now in place, ready for implementation. The tasks for this plan include:

- SEO/keyword testing
- Developing multiple landing pages
- Finalizing our sales format
- Subscriber communications
- Budgeting and metrics
- Advisory board tasking
- Future enhancements
- And, of course, selling it!

By the time you are reading this, *Growthbook* will be in active use. Acquire the app, use the program, and let this author know your thoughts, ideas, updates, etc. The four of us, the start-up entrepreneurs, hope you follow and subscribe to *Growthbook*.

Looking Ahead to Accelerator 20: Manage Your Inner Rainmaker

There are four main cycles to selling: problem, solution, marketing, and messaging. Take the cost of client acquisition into consideration while illustrating survival rates for start-ups. Properly dealing with "nos" provides an unexpected opportunity.

ACCELERATOR 20

Manage Your Rainmaking

I N THIS ACCELERATOR, we will focus on reviewing several key points covered earlier in order to ensure you will apply the tactics and approaches during your sales efforts. We will also include an overview of obstacles you will be facing, especially early in your sales activity.

An entrepreneur's goal, after all their hard work developing their product/service, is to now become a "rainmaker." Once you have the product/service available to sell and deliver to customers, closing sales becomes your major task. As I learned from that first sales experience, speaking-to-selling in front of 300 senior executives, it requires training and active selling. Your success depends on it.

Take the following actions to now begin accelerating your success:

- Use the simplified tools this book provides in leading you to successful sales.
- Make sure you are concentrating on what really works in the real world.

- Use our visual sales tracking system, the Accelerator Funnel, to uncomplicate your sales efforts.
- Finally, hold to a sense of humor, not only internally but when in a sales/prospecting setting.

Early Survival Rate for Start-Ups

Rainmaking for many new entrepreneurs and start-ups may be the second most difficult step, after obtaining financing. Consider the following information a "dose of reality."

According to the *2020 National Report on Early-Stage Entrepreneurship in the United States*, the "early survival rate" of start-ups between 2012 and 2020 averages just under 20%.[27] Put in other terms, approximately 80% of all start-ups fail.

The reasons the majority of start-ups fail vary widely. No two failures happen the exact same way. The British Business Bank goes into more detail on its website with this post:

The 10 Biggest Start-up Challenges
1. Failure to plan
2. Lack of demand
3. Ineffective marketing
4. Knowledge and skills gaps
5. Financial management
6. Securing funding
7. Hiring the right people
8. Leadership
9. Time management and productivity
10. Impact on your health[28]

> **❝Too many firms are managed by consensus or collegiality, not strong decision making.❞**
>
> —Bryan Heathman,
> CEO and Founder of
> Made for Success Publishing

The challenges for start-ups not only involve the business as a whole; many would be considered more individual or "personal" obstacles. Serenity Gibbons identifies a helpful list of these in her October 20, 2020, article "7 Obstacles That Prevent People from Starting Businesses (And How to Overcome Them)" on *Forbes.com*:

1. Financial limitations
2. Inexperience
3. No standout idea
4. Current responsibilities
5. Fear of failure
6. Aversion to stress and hard work
7. Poor timing[29]

Now that we've looked at the challenges in starting a business, let's move back to the positives that will help create success.

> **❝When something is important enough, we should do it even when the odds are against us.❞**
>
> —Elon Musk

A closer view of the positive approaches and tactics to drive your sales efforts follows. According to David Ochi, sales should be a never-ending cycle, consisting of four main cycle segments:

- Problem: What are you trying to solve with your new product/service?
- Solution: The solution should be described in your Unique Selling Proposition (USP).
- Marketing: What tactics and systems will you select to raise awareness, persuade prospects to buy, and remind viewers of the value brought to their need and use?
- Messaging: Select key sales messages to be used throughout all the media used.

In fact, Ochi believes in identifying the market before starting on a project or new product. By finding and validating a problem, then beginning to develop a new product or service, you will be offering a "solution validation."

Then build it, finance it, market it, and sell it. But whether you are busy in your garage developing something new or are a reader taking the lean approach, the 21 accelerators discussed in this book will take you from product conception to the sale.

❝Build a competitive edge.❞
—Frank Mims V,
Mims Morning Meeting

Rainmaking is really what you are about, pouring rain for an accelerated period of time. Let's review several of the best practices from many of our accelerators to make things happen.

- Remember the competencies that Steven Venokur suggested in Accelerator 5? If you believe you have them, strengthen them. If they are missing from your skill set, work on them.
  - o Self-reliance
  - o Adaptability
  - o Critical thinking
  - o Decision making
  - o Initiative
  - o Persistence
  - o Idea generation
  - o Leadership
  - o Resourcefulness
  - o Work organization
  - o Sales

- Network early in the development process of your new service or product. In fact, you should already be networking with community and business groups. Begin talking with them as a way to test the market for your product, even before you begin building it.

66When you work on your network, your network works for you. 99
—Harvey MacKay

- Ensure you have internal management and accountability. If you are selling on your own, trying to generate new business, or if you have a team of only two, make sure you hold each accountable for commitments and follow-up. It is tough. It is demanding. But it is also necessary to grow the kind of business you are really chasing.

- Have a leader for each client and each prospect. If you do have a team of two or more salespeople, designate a leader for each customer and prospect. Your team members may each have multiple numbers of responsibilities.

**❝Effective leadership is putting things first.
Effective management is discipline, carrying it out.❞**

—Stephen Covey

- Each member of your team must have a Revenue Plan. Just as you have developed your accelerator funnel and placed your top 10 priorities in it, make sure your team members do so as well. Ensure that two people are not chasing the same client or prospect.
- Know how many contacts your team is making each week. Every Friday or Saturday morning, review the numbers. Keep a simple lead tracker in the format we suggest. This review will only take five minutes but is essential to do.
- Hold strategy debates before each meeting or before finalizing a proposal. Practice, practice, practice. Part of that practicing is a strategic debate among your team members about how to approach certain issues and certain problems with consistency.
- Is it being used? Once your service or product has been sold and installed, check back frequently to make sure it is being used. As Bill Aulet states in *Disciplined Entrepreneurship,*

66Show that the dogs will eat the dog food.99[30]

You will need to demonstrate to new prospects that your product or service is working successfully and perhaps ask one of your early users/endorsers to serve as a reference.

- Remember to maximize rejection. As Accelerator 4 discussed, if you can ultimately convert only 10% of your "no's" into "yesses," those successes will go directly to your ROI. Remind team members to be tracking different industries' trends and share what they have learned with their colleagues.

   Make this part of the weekly sales meetings since understanding the events in all realms of business may offer spill over to team members in different industries.

- Creative Abandonment, Peter Drucker's management tool we first mentioned in Accelerator 4, offers a unique view of your organization's sales assets and whether they are producing or not. If a proposal is not closing, decide whether it can be refreshed or if it is time to abandon it and move on.

66Rainmaking begins under your own roof.99

Finally, as you are out there pitching, following up, tracking leads, and offering proposals, remember this quote from Coach Jimmy Valvano: "Don't give up. Don't ever give up."

At this point in the book, you are out there prospecting in front of people on your Accelerator Funnel list. You and your team are actively pursuing new business. So, as Sir Richard Branson says, "Engage, engage, engage."

Accelerator 20 Checklist

1. What are the main cycle segments of the "never-ending sales cycle"?
2. Have you begun using the Accelerator Funnel by placing your contacts and prospects onto it?
3. How many of the "entrepreneurial competencies" do you have, and where can you obtain counseling for the others?
4. Have you finalized Product, Place, Promotion, and Price?
5. What is your customer acquisition cost?
6. Remember Coach Valvano's message!

Looking Ahead to Accelerator 21: Build It, Finance It, Market It, Sell It

We have taken all of the recommended actions in the book and present a highly organized Success Map for you to follow to build your sales and reach a high level of success.

ACCELERATOR 21

Build It, Finance It, Market It, Sell It

THINK OF YOUR business like a hot-air balloon. While it's still tied to the ground, it can only rise so high. It has to burn fuel to stay just a few feet above the ground. But once you cut loose the tether, it can rocket to the sky, go for miles, and grow. Like the hot-air balloon costing fuel at first without going anywhere, your business in its fledging stages may feel that way, too. It takes a lot of mental energy, a big learning curve, and persistence to get it to where it starts to pay off.

Whether you are busy in your garage or are just beginning to assess the potential market, these 21 Accelerators will take you from inception to successful sales. As Bryan Heathman stated earlier,

> **66[These Accelerators] have been designed to help you move from churning product development to churning revenue development.99**

Having advised or mentored over 100 start-ups, I recognized early on that a key to entrepreneurs' future success was for them to begin thinking about their next steps while still developing their product or service. Therefore, as presented to you earlier, remember your Success Roadmap helps you in three major ways:

- Making your efforts more productive.
- Helping you concentrate on what really works.
- Providing a simple visual system to set and track prospecting and results.

During the development stages of your great idea, you should now begin studying the market, as David Ochi explained in Accelerator 19. Use the simple, non-time-consuming approaches we have suggested. These will place you in a position to make that future product/service of yours successful.

Customize Your Success Roadmap

To build a measurable roadmap, use all the accelerators, which together provide turn-by-turn guidance and show the most direct route from product/service development to selling prospects. Focus on our succinctly stated Closers Four Growth Keys:

- Find 'em
- Meet 'em
- Get 'em
- Keep 'em

A summary of your roadmap's stops along the way includes:

- Developing your brand and "takeaway" message
- Sharpening your listening skills

- Knowing their businesses
- Prioritizing building relationships
- Financing and accessing capital
- Using the Accelerator Funnel
- Recognizing what works and does not work in selling
- Dealing with "nos"
- Navigating after-sale communications

Recall from Accelerator 17 this quote from Mary Barra, CEO and president of General Motors: "People will do the what if they understand the why." You should now understand the "why" of actively moving from product/service development to sales. Here's how:

Build "It" Now: Nine Steps to Sales Action

- **First Step:** Determine your very first asset, your **brand** or "takeaway" message. Focus specifically on the prospect or client you are addressing. No matter what else people remember or don't remember from the meeting or conversation, it must be this core message. As you progress into your marketing phase, and ultimately into sales, the brand becomes more critical.

   Remember, a brand is not a logo. It is not an isolated image. It is the feeling or the essence of what you are producing that will ultimately resonate with future buyers.

- **Second Step:** Listening must permeate sales. Next to your "takeaway" message, the art of listening is the most important, effective tool in a pitch meeting. By combining the two, the frequency of your takeaway message and listening carefully to what is being said, you will open up a major roadway to gaining new business.

In the questions you develop, show what you have learned about the company/firm/non-profit. Listen carefully to their answers. In turn, this provides you with an understanding of their needs, values, and how to react to winning their business.

Remember to get them talking.

- **Third Step:** You and your team need to **know their business**. Make sure you learn ahead of that first meeting who their primary and secondary competitors are. Understand what is going on in their industry and whether products or services similar to what they make are in development elsewhere.

  As you get to know the inside contact, ask about internal pressures they may be facing. Do they have personal goals to be moving up in their current organization, or are they looking to transfer elsewhere? You might even be able to serve as a reference for them.

- **Fourth Step:** The priority of always **building relationships** (ABR) should begin early in the development phase of your new product or service. Tactics and techniques we suggest are designed to help you (and your team) get to know clients and prospects. These techniques will help them know and trust you. We cannot say it enough to keep on building relationships.

  View their needs first. For example, learn what type of communications they want from you and how they prefer to communicate back. Are emails, Zooms, text, or phone preferred? If there is a problem, fix it, fix it fast, and then remind them periodically how you responded.

  Reach out for that handshake and smile.

- **Fifth Step:** Looking for necessary **financing** and accessing capital should also begin early in your development phase. Without some type of track record, this may be the single greatest obstacle a new start-up might face. Even if you have prepared all the requirements a specific funding source requires, it is not easy. Only a small portion of start-ups and new entrepreneurs are able to gain financing.

  A main focus of this book is to move new entrepreneurs out of the "garage" and the intense focus on the new product or service where they are not thinking ahead. When you ultimately realize you need financing and don't know where to go, "get your house in order."

  From undertaking a business plan to organizing the necessary documents, finding an intermediary to assist in this search is typically the necessary way to go.

- **Sixth Step:** Once you have begun moving into the marketing phase, use our **Accelerator Funnel** on a daily basis. This simple visual tool is designed to help you build a base of prospects, customers/clients, and referrals, set sales priorities, and close new business. It will keep you on track with an easy-to-read status report.

  By prioritizing customers/clients, prospects, and referrals, and adding to each group as marketing and selling is activated, you will be rapidly growing a base for future client acquisition.

  Start with prospects you know. Focus on quick wins. Help anyone working with you to do the same thing. It will make you feel better and encourage your selling successes.

- **Seventh Step:** Make sure you (and your team) fully understand **what does work and what does not work in selling**. Over many years, my team members and I have talked with clients and seminar attendees about what offends them in sales meetings. Ensure that your team does not make mistakes and presents positive attitudes. These are critical to building trust.

  Trust builds sales. It drives expectations that your prospects will need in order to repeat orders and refer you to others. Business ethics is one of those considerations salespeople often overlook. This is usually not deliberate. However, dealing with issues that occasionally arise when trying to close a deal could lead to clouded thinking and an inappropriate response.

- **Eighth Step: Dealing with "nos"** is one of those bumps along the way. If you have lost a pitch, an RFP competition, or a new client/customer, it never feels good. When this happens, think about it this way: The prospect cared enough to meet with you, spend time with you, and consider your product or service. Hopefully, you were able to have them exchange ideas and options with you and perhaps got so far as reviewing a proposal.

  Don't discard their decision. Instead, put them on the lower end of your Accelerator Funnel priority list. Think about maximizing that rejection. Stay in touch with those "nos" on a regular basis, and you might ultimately win new business.

- **Ninth Step: After-sale communications** once you have landed a contract are as important, if not more important, to keep that client/customer. Make sure they are using what you sold to them as an easy communication tactic. Let them know what you and your company are currently engaged in and ask for their ideas and questions.

As for the work you are currently undertaking for them, communicate the next steps and keep them informed of any changes they or you believe are necessary. Ask about the challenges they are facing and offer assistance. Be aware of your relationships and be on the lookout for subtle changes.

While client dissatisfaction is never comfortable to deal with, it is something you should be aware of long before a client disengages. Even if it seems insignificant, when even the smallest issue arises, deal with it immediately.

Take action and win them back.

My Best Wishes to You

By now, you are way past the tipping point. Even if you have had no sales experience, by following this Success Roadmap and using our robust 21 Accelerators, you will be growing a sales pipeline.

It is my hope that you can ease the transition from building the new product or service to successfully selling it. This book is designed to make the pathway from applying basic skills and tactics to successfully generating revenue.

I've gone through this process myself. Fortunately, along the way, I've encountered three mentors who have redirected me at just the right times. Now in my work as an entrepreneurial mentor and advisor, it's been as much an education for me as for them.

We included in this book a history of a current start-up three of my colleagues and I are building, as well as a look at our publisher's own start-up in order for you to see firsthand

and in real-time our struggles, obstacles, challenges, wrong turns, and real opportunities. Use your resourcefulness, initiative, and problem-solving skills to thrive.

I'm with you all the way.
Allan Colman

ABOUT THE AUTHOR

D R. ALLAN COLMAN understands the challenges facing both established businesses and entrepreneurs. He has advised organization leaders from 10 to 15,000 employees, focusing on small to mid-sized groups. In addition to customizing strategic action plans to fit size and industry, he has also been the chief executive of a 5,600-employee public agency.

Colman is known for his passion in building stronger, more effective organizations and for his ability to help companies and firms quickly achieve their growth goals. He has spent more than three decades assisting in and working for companies and firms, helping to bring in millions of dollars in new revenue and building leadership structures that continue to perform. Allan is currently the Adjunct Professor of Marketing at California State University Dominguez Hills.

Allan and Robin continue living and enjoying Southern California and are proud parents of 2 "very adult" daughters, Tyson and Brittany.

ENDNOTES

[1] Hogle, Scott. *Persuade: The 7 Empowering Laws of the Salesmaker*. P. 102.

[2] Abraham, Jay. *Getting Everything You Can Out of All You've Got*.

[3] Abraham, Jay. *Getting Everything You Can Out of All You've Got*.

[4] Abraham, Jay. *Getting Everything You Can Out of All You've Got*.

[5] Abraham, Jay. *Getting Everything You Can Out of All You've Got*.

[6] Robbins, Tony and Holmes, Chet. *Business Breakthroughs*.

[7] Robbins, Tony and Holmes, Chet. *Business Breakthroughs*.

[8] Yolanda Guibert article? Blog post?

[9] Colman, Allan. *Lead Like a Boss*.

[10] PricewaterhouseCoopers January 2021 survey

[11] American Marketing Association Statement of Ethics 2014.

[12] Manahan, Michael S. *Secrets to Raising Capital*, 2nd edition.

[13] Polk, Gary and Brodmann, Jennifer. *Why Women Entrepreneurs Fail (To Win)*.

[14] 2020 Women Entrepreneurship Report

[15] Aulet, Bill. *Discipled Entrepreneurship*.

[16] Perreault, Cannon, and McCarthy. *Essentials of Marketing*.

[17] Hogle, Scott. *Persuade: The 7 Empowering Laws of the SalesMaker*.

[18] Miniere, Thomas. YEC Council post, accessed Nov. 1, 2021.

[19] "Sales." *Wikipedia*. Accessed Nov. 1, 2021.

[20] Heathman, Bryan. *Conversion Marketing*.

[21] Harvard Business Publication.
[22] Abraham, Jay. *Getting Everything You Can Out of All You've Got.*
[23] Heathman, Bryan. *Conversion Marketing.*
[24] Hogle, Scott. *Persuade.*
[25] Hogle, Scott. *Persuade.*
[26] Perrault, Cannon & McCarthy. *Essentials of Marketing.*
[27] 2020 National Report on Early-Stage Entrepreneurship in the United States
[28] The British Bank
[29] https://www.forbes.com/sites/serenitygibbons/2020/10/20/7-obstacles-that-prevent-people-from-starting-businesses-and-how-to-overcome-them/?sh=40b7368b3064
[30] Aulet, Bill. *Disciplined Entrepreneurship.* Wiley 2013.

ACKNOWLEDGEMENTS

I T IS SO hard to believe that in the most intensive three days of planning, sales expert Scott Hogle, President of iHeart Radio Honolulu, and Bryan Heathman, CEO of Made for Success, helped me work through a format that ended with 21 Accelerators. From identifying the people who need the most start-up help, to the solutions that would assist them the most, to the book's format that would make the learning process work, Scott and Bryan drove this project forward. My job became the simplest, write the book! I will be forever grateful.

The Made for Success team edited, refreshed, organized, tracked, and pushed me when needed. DeeDee, Kristin, Alice, Kyle, Tyler, and various pet dogs, kept the project on time and on focus. There is no better publishing team.

All of us never lost sight of thousands of start-up entrepreneurs, busy working in their garages, to bring something new, positive, dynamic, and helpful. We are with you all the way.

ACCELERATOR ACTION LIST BY CHAPTER

Accelerator #1

5 Keys to Determine Value

Accelerator #2

5 Clues to Knowing Their Business
One Size Does Not Fit All

Accelerator #3

9 Clues to Knowing Thy Client
Relationship Killers

Accelerator #5

7 Steps to Building Relationships
15 Attributes the Naked Entrepreneur Must Possess
10 Attributes Need of All Entrepreneurs
11 Mistakes That Offend Businesspeople

Accelerator #6

8 Requirements to Get Your House in Order
Sources of Private Equity and Capital
Secrets to Raising Capital
Case Study: 8 Closing Skills

Accelerator #8

5 Questions for Creating Your (USP) Unique Selling Proposition

Accelerator #9

5 Types of Joint Ventures
Business Strengths
Industry Attractiveness
Partnership Agreement Elements

Accelerator #10

6 Characteristics of Good Leadership
15 Pre-Meeting Questions
Hogle's 5 Rules of Focused Learning

Accelerator #11

Top 3 Marketing Myths
10 Types of Marketing
4 Hidden Sales Tools for Marketing

Accelerator #12

14 Best Closing Skills Practices

Accelerator #13

5 Keys to Successful Marketing
21 Keys to Driving Performance

Accelerator #14

Top 6 Tactics for Successful Prospect Engagements
12 Kickass Revenue Signals
Why Should I Hire You? 13 Questions

Accelerator #16

8 Actions To Keeping Customers
23 Growth Actions

Accelerator #17

Self-Sabotaging Excuses for Not Selling
10 Agonizing Excuses for Not Selling

Accelerator #18

9 Ways to Avoid Driving Clients Crazy
12 Essential Practices for Revenue Growth

Accelerator #20

10 Biggest Start-Up Challenges

Accelerator #21

Your Roadmap's 9 Stops
9 Steps to Sales Action